T0316543

Cambridge Elements

Elements in Reinventing Capitalism
edited by
Arie Y. Lewin
Duke University
Till Talaulicar
University of Erfurt

FROM FINANCIALISATION TO INNOVATION IN UK BIG PHARMA

AstraZeneca and GlaxoSmithKline

Öner Tulum
The Academic-Industry Research Network
Antonio Andreoni
SOAS University of London
William Lazonick
The Academic-Industry Research Network

Shaftesbury Road, Cambridge CB2 8EA, United Kingdom

One Liberty Plaza, 20th Floor, New York, NY 10006, USA

477 Williamstown Road, Port Melbourne, VIC 3207, Australia

314–321, 3rd Floor, Plot 3, Splendor Forum, Jasola District Centre,
New Delhi – 110025, India

103 Penang Road, #05–06/07, Visioncrest Commercial, Singapore 238467

Cambridge University Press is part of Cambridge University Press & Assessment,
a department of the University of Cambridge.

We share the University's mission to contribute to society through the pursuit of
education, learning, and research at the highest international levels of excellence.

www.cambridge.org
Information on this title: www.cambridge.org/9781009278164

DOI: 10.1017/9781009278140

First published 2022

A catalogue record for this publication is available from the British Library.

ISBN 978-1-009-27816-4 Paperback
ISSN 2634-8950 (online)
ISSN 2634-8942 (print)

From Financialisation to Innovation in UK Big Pharma

AstraZeneca and GlaxoSmithKline

Elements in Reinventing Capitalism

DOI: 10.1017/9781009278140
First published online: November 2022

Öner Tulum
The Academic-Industry Research Network

Antonio Andreoni
SOAS University of London

William Lazonick
The Academic-Industry Research Network

Author for correspondence: Öner Tulum, onertulum@gmail.com

Abstract: The tension between innovation and financialisation is central to the business corporation. Innovation entails a 'retain-and-reinvest' allocation regime that can form a foundation for stable and equitable economic growth. Driven by shareholder-value ideology, financialisation entails a shift to 'downsize-and-distribute'. This Element investigates this tension in global pharmaceuticals, focusing on the two leading UK companies AstraZeneca (AZN) and GlaxoSmithKline (GSK). In the 2000s, both adopted US-style governance, including stock buybacks and stock-based executive pay. Over the past decade, however, first AZN and then GSK transitioned to innovation. Critical was the cessation of buybacks to refocus capabilities on investing in an innovative drugs pipeline. Enabling this shift were UK corporate-governance institutions that mitigated US-style shareholder-value maximisation. Reinventing capitalism for the sake of stable and equitable economic growth means eliminating value destruction caused by financialisation and supporting value creation through collective and cumulative innovation. This title is also available as Open Access on Cambridge Core.

Keywords: financialisation, innovation, pharmaceutical industry, GlaxoSmithKline, AstraZeneca

ISBNs: 9781009278164 (PB), 9781009278140 (OC)
ISSNs: 2634-8950 (online), 2634-8942 (print)

Contents

1 Introduction

This Element investigates the tension between innovation and financialisation in the global pharmaceutical industry, with a focus on two leading UK companies – AstraZeneca (AZN) and GlaxoSmithKline (GSK) – from the time of the mergers that created them (1999 and 2000, respectively) to the present. The tension between innovation and financialisation is central to modern capitalism and its capacity to deliver sustainable prosperity. Overall, financialisation reflects the rise of shareholder-value ideology and the resulting shift from a 'retain-and-reinvest' to a 'downsize-and-distribute' resource-allocation regime. Financialisation manifests differently across enterprises, industries, and economies.

Against this backdrop, and drawing on other empirical works conducted by various authors over the years, we place the study of these two UK-based companies in the context of innovation and competition among twenty Big Pharma companies based in Europe and the United States. We argue that companies that mitigate financialisation and support innovation perform better in global competition. This conclusion may seem obvious to those who understand the critical importance of dynamic capabilities for competitive performance, but it is not at all obvious to those financial economists, corporate executives, and hedge-fund managers who argue that 'maximising shareholder value' (MSV) promotes superior economic performance. In our view, a critique of this flawed ideology through industry studies is central to 'reinventing capitalism', especially in the context of the health industry and its impact on human well-being.

Our comparative study of AZN and GSK is part of that research agenda and provides new evidence for informing concrete sets of corporate-governance reforms. Using 'the theory of innovative enterprise' framework, through empirical studies such as the ones offered in this Element, we analyse the interaction of strategy, organisation, and finance at each of the companies. The evidence we collect is new and updated to early 2022. Our analysis speaks to recent discussions on 'stakeholder capitalism' and 'rethinking the purpose of the corporation', especially in key industries such as health.

We have found that in the decade after their mergers both companies adopted US-style governance models, manifested by stock buybacks, in addition to dividends, and US-style stock-based pay, which rewarded senior executives for boosting the company's stock price, even if the price increases were driven by manipulation (via buybacks) and speculation rather than innovation. In the aftermath of the 2008–9 financial crisis, however, key directors and shareholders in both companies began to rethink their business models, with AZN decisively shifting from financialisation to innovation in 2013 with the appointment of Pascal Soriot as CEO. Central to this transition was the cessation of buybacks in order to focus as many resources as possible, including executive attention, on investing in the drugs pipeline. This process continues at AZN and is a prime reason why it was chosen to partner with Oxford University in the development, manufacture, and delivery of the COVID-19 vaccine. It took GSK a few years longer to begin transitioning from financialisation to innovation, with the reorientation of the company's focus towards innovation becoming more evident when Emma Walmsley replaced Andrew Witty as CEO in March 2017, with buybacks ceasing completely in 2018.

Our study also uncovers important differences in corporate-governance institutions in the United Kingdom from those which prevail in the United States. The UK institutions, expressed in part in the UK Corporate Governance Code, ultimately provided support to AZN and GSK in shifting from financialisation to innovation. Like the United States, the United Kingdom has a shareholder model of capitalism, but, in part because of British business reactions to the extreme US orientation towards MSV from the late 1980s, the UK governance institutions include defences against financialisation that are not present in the United States. We raise these issues in the conclusion of the study to argue that, despite globalisation, 'reinventing capitalism' still needs to recognise the importance of national institutions.

2 Innovation and Competition in the Global Pharmaceutical Industry

Within any business firm, there is a resource-allocation tension between innovation and financialisation. Innovation entails the generation of a product that is of higher quality and lower cost than the previously available one (Lazonick 2019a). In the pharmaceutical industry, the measures of higher quality are the safety and effectiveness of a medicine. The availability of a safer and more effective medicine enables the pharmaceutical company to access a large extent of the market (i.e., patients whose health can be improved by taking the drug), thus transforming the high fixed cost of developing the safer and more effective drug into a low unit cost. The lower unit cost is the result of 'economies of scale', which means that the drug has been made more accessible to patients. A lower unit cost can also permit lower pricing of the medicine to make it more affordable to patients. Alternatively, a higher drug price can provide the pharmaceutical company with higher profits that can be reinvested in drug innovation (Collington and Lazonick 2022).

Given existing and new medical needs, the development of a safe and effective medicine requires investment in the productive capabilities of people who can engage in organisational learning within research labs operated by government, business, and civil society organisations. For a drug developer, the implementation of an innovation strategy requires investment in teams of researchers who have specialised knowledge, acquired much more through work experience than through advanced formal education (as necessary as higher education is in this industry). This accumulation of unique knowledge occurs at the discovery stage, through clinical trials, in the drug manufacturing process, and from data collected of an approved medicine in use.

A pharmaceutical firm's innovative capabilities reside largely in its human resources. With the rapid advancement of technology within the pharmaceutical industry, drug development using novel methods has tended to be done by start-ups, the most successful of which are highly focused on new areas of specialised learning. Once an innovative company has a successful product, its senior executives may allocate the firm's resources to further investments in organisational learning that, for the sake of developing a new round of innovative products, builds on the specialised knowledge that it has accumulated. Key to the success of these investments in human capabilities is 'organisational integration': the enabling, coordinating, and incentivising of large numbers of people with different functional specialties and hierarchical responsibilities to devote their skills and efforts to the innovation process.

Through sustained innovation across generations of products, a small pharmaceutical company can grow to be large as a distinct business firm, or what can be called a unit of strategic control. Alternatively, by selling itself or merging with another company, its further growth may occur as part of another unit of strategic control. The success or failure of a merger or acquisition will depend on the organisational integration of the employees of the two business units into the unified firm that now exercises strategic control.

The growth of the pharmaceutical firm requires sustained commitment of financial resources to an innovation process that is *collective*, *cumulative*, and *uncertain*. It is collective because it entails the organisational integration of large teams of people. It is *cumulative* because what the organisation learned yesterday provides a foundation for what it is capable of learning today. It is uncertain because the investments in organisational learning may fail to develop a safe and effective medicine.

Hence, in exercising strategic control, the abilities and incentives of senior pharmaceutical executives are of critical importance to the allocation of resources to the innovation process. They bear the responsibility to make decisions to invest in certain types of medicines in the face of the uncertainty of whether the firm will be able to develop a higher-quality, lower-cost drug than is currently available. To implement the innovation strategy, they make investments in productive capabilities, largely embodied in people engaged in collective and cumulative learning, that, through organisational integration, can enable these capabilities to generate an innovative product. The most high-powered means of organisational integration is provision of personnel with the sustained employment through which they can accumulate productive capabilities, attain incomes commensurate with those capabilities, and build rewarding careers.

This organisational-learning process unfolds over time from the point at which investments in innovation are made to the point at which a commercial product, if it is indeed generated, can result in financial returns. Early drug development has three distinct stages: *target identification*, *lead identification*, and *lead optimisation*. During the target-identification stage, scientists engage in extensive learning to gain insight into the biology and mechanism of a disease of interest. Enhanced understanding of the disease mechanism enables drug discovery efforts to focus on lead identification of potential targets in the disease mechanism. In this stage, drug discovery efforts also concentrate on identifying the number of potential leads (chemical compounds) to pursue as effective pharmaceutical interventions (Figure 1).

Drug safety is a paramount concern for scientists to address in the lead-optimisation stage when designing compounds that are intended for long-term use. Scientists may choose to bring several variations of a lead compound as backups to be further examined during preclinical studies outside (in vitro) or inside (in vivo) living organisms. Engaging in deep learning to better understand a disease during the early discovery stages has major implications for preclinical and clinical stages of the drug-development process. Any increase in the number of lead compounds advancing into the preclinical stage can potentially undermine the productivity of the entire drug-development effort and

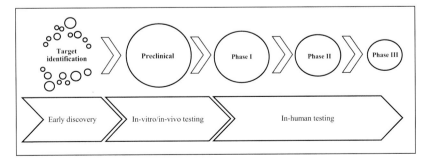

Figure 1 Drug discovery process
Source: Authors' own illustration.

result in an increased compound failure rate in the preclinical or first-in-human toxicology testing phases.

To sustain this innovation process until it results in financial returns, executives who exercise strategic control mobilise funds that provide financial commitment. In the pharmaceutical industry, start-ups are typically financed by venture capital, which can 'exit' from its investment (often before the firm has even generated a commercial product) through a listing on a stock exchange (of which NASDAQ is the most important) or through the sale of the company to an established firm (Lazonick and Tulum 2011). In pharmaceuticals, as in any other industry, once the firm has generated profitable products, the net income that it retains becomes the foundation of financial commitment.

Through this process of retaining profits and reinvesting in productive capabilities, both internally and through strategic acquisitions, it is possible for an innovative enterprise to grow to become a multi-product pharmaceutical company, with the capability of developing more complex drugs. The most successful companies also invest in manufacturing and marketing capabilities, including committing resources to specialised productive assets and facilities (Chang and Andreoni 2020). A fully integrated pharmaceutical company can grow to employ tens of thousands of highly qualified and well-paid personnel, who then, through stable employment and promotion opportunities, can become more experienced and productive over the course of their careers. In the global medicinal drug industry, these types of firms, many of them dating back a century or more, have become known as 'Big Pharma'.[1]

There is always the possibility, however, that the executives who exercise strategic control over a firm that has become profitable through innovation may decide to allocate its enhanced cash flow to a process that we call 'financialisation': the extraction of value from the firm for the benefit of certain parties above and beyond rewards justified by the contributions that these parties have made to the value-creating processes that have resulted in innovation and profits (Lazonick and Shin 2020). It can be the case that certain groups of powerful employees are the beneficiaries of financialisation; historically, across a range of industries, trade unions have often been blamed (whether deservedly or not) for using their collective power to bargain for pay and benefits that exceed their value-creating contributions.

In the twenty-first century, however, these 'value-extracting' employees are more likely to be senior corporate executives, enriched by stock-based pay and lavish pensions. In the name of MSV, these value-extracting executives bestow

---

[1] Big Pharma is a term that refers collectively to a small number of large, established global pharmaceutical companies that engage in manufacturing and marketing in addition to R&D.

benefits on shareholders, including themselves, in the form of cash dividends and share repurchases. In addition, stock traders, who acquire corporate shares on the stock market, may be able to assert their power over corporate resource allocation for the sake of value extraction, achieved by timing the selling of the shares that they previously purchased (Lazonick 2019b; Lazonick and Shin 2020). The value extracted by these executives and traders is often far in excess of any contributions that they have made to the firm's value-creating process.

This value extraction takes the form of the yields on the company's stock, enhanced by cash dividends and share repurchases (aka stock buybacks). As we explain in this Element, stock buybacks done as open-market repurchases are a much more deleterious mode of financialisation than dividends. All shareholders of a class of stock benefit from dividends by *holding* shares. In contrast, the purpose of buybacks done as open-market repurchases is generally to manipulate the company's stock price to reward well-positioned stock traders for *selling*, not holding, shares in the company.

In the extreme, when the company downsizes its labour force, divests production capacity, and takes on debt for the sake of increasing payouts to shareholders, corporate resource allocation becomes what Lazonick and Shin (2020) call 'predatory value extraction'. In their analysis, based on recent US experience, predatory value extraction results from the combined power of corporate managers as value-extracting insiders, asset managers as value-extracting enablers, and hedge-fund managers as value-extracting outsiders, operating in a national institutional environment that permits, and even encourages, this value-extracting activity (Lazonick 2018; Lazonick and Shin 2020; Lazonick and Jacobson 2022).

In the world of Big Pharma, extreme financialisation undermines the processes of drug innovation and the sustainability of the firm as an innovative enterprise. By the same token, those major pharmaceutical companies that have resisted financialisation have emerged as or remained global leaders in drug innovation (Lazonick and Tulum 2011; Tulum 2018; Tulum and Lazonick 2018; Lazonick et al. 2019). As shown in Table 1, in 2020, the world's ten largest companies in the global pharmaceutical industry generated 50 per cent of the industry's revenues. The two leaders, Roche and Novartis, both based in Switzerland, are, like most Europe-based pharmaceutical firms, less-financialised companies than their US-based competitors such as Merck and Pfizer. Nevertheless, Novartis is much more financialised than Roche. Less-financialised companies have gained market share in global pharmaceuticals (Tulum and Lazonick 2018; Lazonick et al. 2019).

Table 1 Worldwide prescription drug sales, top ten companies, and national bases, 2021

Company	National base	Worldwide prescription drug sales, $billions	Worldwide market share, percentage
AbbVie	USA	56.2	5.9
Roche	Switzerland	49.2	5.2
Novartis	Switzerland	42.0	4.4
Johnson & Johnson	USA	52.1	5.5
Merck & Co.	USA	42.8	4.5
Sanofi	France	37.7	4.0
Pfizer	USA	79.6	8.4
Bristol-Myers Squibb	USA	45.1	4.7
AstraZeneca	UK and Sweden	36.5	3.9
GlaxoSmithKline	UK	33.1	3.5
Top ten worldwide sales total		**474.1**	**50.0**
All pharma worldwide sales total		**949.0**	**100.0**

Source: Authors' calculations are based on company annual reports and Evaluate Pharma, World Preview 2021, Outlook to 2026, 14th edition, July 2021.

In this Element, we focus on the two UK-based companies in the top ten: AZN and GSK. Given the extreme financialisation of US Big Pharma companies (Tulum and Lazonick 2018; Lazonick et al. 2019), which make up 50 per cent of the world's top ten, it is of great importance to the global pharmaceutical industry as well as to the innovative capability of the UK economy that these two UK-based companies avoid the adoption of the US business model. This Element provides an in-depth analysis of the evolving tension between innovation and financialisation at AZN and GSK from the time of the mergers in 1999 and 2000, respectively, to the present.

The key findings of our study, which we document in detail in this Element, are that, influenced by US-style corporate governance, both AZN and GSK became more financialised in the decade after the mergers that formed them, but, then, over the course of the following decade both companies altered their resource-allocation strategies to shift away from financialisation towards innovation. Our analysis of the processes of corporate-governance transformation at AZN and GSK provides unique insights into the UK institutional environment relevant to corporate governance. It also sheds light on the ways in which UK corporate-governance institutions differ from those in the United States, where, as we have shown, predatory value extraction has become the norm (Tulum and Lazonick 2018; Lazonick et al. 2019; Lazonick and Shin 2020; Lazonick 2022a).

The United Kingdom derives several benefits from the existence and persistence of these two UK-based companies as innovative competitors in the global pharmaceutical industry. According to the most recent data, AZN employs 8,300 people from seventy nations at its UK sites (AstraZeneca 2021). As can be seen in Table 2, AZN has been increasing the number of UK employees since 2017 as part of its global expansion. In 2021, GSK employed 16,000 people at eighteen UK sites (GSK 2021). Table 2 also shows GSK's total employment from 1997 to 2021.

The presence of major global competitors in the United Kingdom provides the government with a rationale for investing in the advanced-technology knowledge base (O'Sullivan et al. 2013; BEIS 2017; BEIS 2021). Some of the scientists who gain experience at these large companies leave to form new ventures, and we can assume that those who gain career experience and establish social connections while working in the United Kingdom are more likely to seek out entrepreneurial opportunities there. The COVID-19 pandemic has demonstrated the importance of both AZN and GSK to the United Kingdom's participation in the global vaccine response. GSK is one of only four Big Pharma companies (along with Merck, Pfizer, and Sanofi) that possessed vaccine capabilities coming into the pandemic. Even though AZN does not have vaccine capabilities, Oxford University chose AZN to manage the manufacture and distribution of its COVID-19 vaccine, in large part because it is UK-based (Tulum et al. 2021).

Given the centrality of mergers and acquisitions (M&A) in the global pharmaceutical industry over the past few decades, the survival of AZN and GSK as UK-based companies was not inevitable. As we document in this Element, complex and intersecting social factors in the global pharmaceutical industry paved the way for the 'merger mania' of the 1990s and early 2000s, and the movements for absorption and concentration continue to have major impacts on the industry (Gagnon and Volesky 2017; Liu 2021). Whether as an attempt to reduce costs or to develop new revenue sources, a proliferation of mergers has transformed the corporate identities, including the national home bases, of leading companies in the global pharmaceutical industry.

The fact is that in 2021 these two UK-based companies were major competitors in the consolidated industry. The merger of Zeneca with Astra occurred in 1999 and that of Glaxo Wellcome with SmithKline Beecham (SKB) in 2000

Table 2 AZN and GSK employees, by geographic area, 1997–2021

	AZN					GSK			
	Global	United Kingdom	Europe	Americas	Rest of world	Global	Europe	USA	Rest of world
Year	FYA thousand	% of global				FYA thousand	% of global		
1999	47.2	20.6	40.7	27.3	11.4	112.9	43.8	19.5	36.7
2000	50.1	20.0	40.7	28.3	11.0	108.3	42.7	21.2	36.1
2001	52.6	19.4	37.8	31.7	11.0	107.5	43.3	22.0	34.8
2002	57.5	18.6	39.3	31.0	11.1	106.0	44.0	22.5	33.4
2003	61.0	18.2	39.2	29.3	13.3	102.7	44.2	23.8	32.0
2004	64.2	17.9	39.9	28.8	13.4	100.5	44.7	23.8	31.6
2005	64.9	17.9	40.4	27.6	14.2	100.4	43.7	23.6	32.7
2006	66.6	17.7	39.9	27.3	15.0	101.7	44.6	24.1	31.4
2007	67.9	17.4	37.7	29.7	15.2	103.1	45.3	24.0	30.7
2008	66.1	16.6	34.9	31.6	16.8	101.2	45.1	21.4	33.5
2009	63.9	16.6	33.2	31.0	19.2	99.5	42.1	22.6	35.3
2010	61.7	16.4	32.6	29.7	21.4	98.2	41.4	18.2	40.4
2011	59.8	14.5	32.1	30.1	23.2	96.9	39.7	17.2	43.1
2012	53.5	14.8	30.1	28.6	26.5	98.4	39.0	17.3	43.7

Table 2 (cont.)

Year	AZN					GSK			
	Global	United Kingdom	Europe	Americas	Rest of world	Global	Europe	USA	Rest of world
	FYA thousand	% of global				FYA thousand	% of global		
2013	51.6	14.0	27.1	28.3	30.6	99.5	38.6	16.6	44.8
2014	55.9	12.9	24.7	30.1	32.4	98.7	38.7	16.9	44.4
2015	60.1	11.8	24.6	29.1	34.4	99.6	43.0	14.5	42.5
2016	61.5	11.4	23.9	28.9	35.8	100.3	42.6	14.6	42.8
2017	60.0	11.5	24.2	27.2	37.2	98.9	43.7	14.8	41.6
2018	63.2	11.4	23.4	26.4	38.8	97.0	43.9	14.5	41.6
2019	67.3	11.0	23.0	24.7	41.3	97.5	40.8	16.8	42.5
2020	74.8	10.6	22.2	23.1	44.1	96.8	43.3	16.7	40.0
2021	79.6	11.2	23.0	23.6	42.2	92.1	43.1	15.9	41.1

Note: Fiscal year average (FYA).

Source: Authors' calculations are based on company annual reports.

(Heracleous and Murray 2001; Quirke and Slinn 2010). At the time, the field for developing novel medicines was becoming crowded as fledgling biotech start-ups raced to capture the seemingly lucrative, and rapidly expanding, market for immunotherapies and other specialty drugs (Pisano 2006, chapters 2 and 3; Lazonick and Tulum 2011; Owen and Hopkins 2016).

Big Pharma was at a competitive disadvantage in terms of possessing the necessary capabilities for developing novel medicines that could address the varied and complex health challenges of the twenty-first century. In particular, the established companies failed to recognise and engage in new learning in the fields of molecular biology during the last three decades of the twentieth century.[2] With the expansion of the start-up sector in the 1980s and 1990s, Big Pharma saw the new ventures as competitors that were luring away key scientists and securing valuable intellectual-property protection.

The flow of human resources and intellectual property to start-ups dissipated Big Pharma's once-formidable capabilities for new drug development. Struggling to overcome this dilemma, in the late 1990s Big Pharma engaged in unprecedented M&A activity that could potentially transform their lacklustre drug-development capabilities (Rafols et al. 2014). Over the past two decades, the financial support and possibility of acquiring innovative new ventures by the established pharmaceutical companies have created a synergistic dynamic between Big Pharma and the start-up sector for drug development and delivery. As we shall see, AZN and GSK have both been able to enhance their drug-development capabilities by the acquisition of young companies located in both the United Kingdom and abroad.

Large numbers of these biopharma start-ups are based in the United States, which is by far the world leader in venture-backed companies (Murphey 2020). Given the proliferation of these start-ups and unregulated drug prices as well as subsidies and market incentives available in the United States, the US pharmaceutical ecosystem provides an ideal environment for a *non-financialised* company that is willing to reinvest its profits in drug development to generate innovation. As Lazonick et al. (2017) argue, however, many US-based pharmaceutical companies have been failing to take advantage of these opportunities because they are highly financialised. Indeed, as a result of their focus on value extraction at the expense of value creation, financialised companies are facing a deep productivity crisis in terms of bringing innovative new therapies to the drug market (Tulum and Lazonick 2018; Lazonick et al. 2019).

---

[2] Drawing on his first-hand experience during his tenure as Amgen's top executive, Gordon Binder explains the difficulties that the company and many other biotech start-ups encountered in the 1980s and 1990s in stimulating the interest of Big Pharma to forge partnerships to develop a new generation of medicines (Binder and Bashe 2008).

Major European pharmaceutical companies, including those based in the United Kingdom, which are subject to price regulation in their home markets, have positioned themselves to tap into the immense knowledge base in the United States and sell innovative products there at high, unregulated prices. The higher profits that they gain from sales in the US market can then be used to develop the next generation of innovative products. Through a listing on the US stock market, pharmaceutical companies can also use their shares as an acquisition currency, in addition to or instead of cash, to gain control of innovative new ventures. As they recruit executives in the United States, these companies might adopt US-style executive compensation systems, emphasising the inflation of stock-based pay through distributions to shareholders, and especially through stock buybacks, which give manipulative boosts to stock prices (Lazonick 2014a, 2015). While expanding their research & development and commercial infrastructures to take advantage of the US innovation system and its large pharmaceutical market, the very participation of these companies in the US pharmaceutical industry may result in their adoption of governance norms and managerial cultures that encourage a shift from innovation to financialisation.[3]

Section 3 of this Element provides our general framework for analysing the tension between innovation and financialisation, based on the theory of innovative enterprise, which focuses on three social conditions: strategic control, organisational integration, and financial commitment. As an empirical point of departure for the analysis of the tension between innovation and financialisation, we provide basic indicators – distributions to shareholders in the form of dividends and buybacks as well as drugs in the pipeline relative to R&D expenditures – for the eight largest US-based and eight largest Europe-based pharmaceutical companies by revenues in 2021. Included among the Europe-based companies are AZN and GSK.

Sections 4 and 5 analyse the evolution of the innovation-financialisation tension at AZN and GSK, respectively, highlighting the different trajectories of the two companies. As in previous work (Tulum 2018; Tulum and Lazonick 2018), the research summarised in this Element shows the importance of in-depth company-level studies of the relation between resource allocation and economic performance, using the 'social conditions of innovative enterprise' framework. The analysis of the dynamic interactions of firm-level strategy, organisation, and finance enables us to comprehend the evolving relation

---

[3] For previous discussions of the financialisation of the pharmaceutical industry in Europe, see Froud et al. 2006, part II, pp. 149–210; Haslam et al. 2013; Montalban and Sakınç 2013; and Gleadle et al. 2014.

between investment in a firm's productive capabilities and its competitive performance as an historical process, brought up to the present.

During the first decade or so after their formation in 1999 and 2000, both AZN and GSK engaged in corporate resource-allocation strategies that entailed financialisation and undermined innovation. If these trajectories had continued over the following decade, it is highly unlikely that either AZN or GSK would still be independent UK-based companies. Especially in the aftermath of the financial crisis of 2008–9, these companies became potential takeover targets – as continues to be the case. In 2014, US-based Pfizer sought to take over AZN, and AZN's successful response in fending off the merger reinforced the resolve of the leadership of the UK company to move from financialisation to innovation. As a UK-based company, AZN has played a central, although at times contentious, role in the COVID-19 vaccine rollout. Beginning in April 2021, GSK, with its stock price down, came under attack from US hedge-fund activist Elliott Management, run by Paul Singer, one of the world's most notorious 'vulture capitalists' (Stone 2013; Kolhatkar 2018).

The final section of this Element takes stock of the evolution of the tension between innovation and financialisation at AZN and GSK, summarising our views of why each of the companies moved towards financialisation in the 2000s but shifted towards innovation in the 2010s. The answers to these questions have policy implications for the design of UK corporate-governance institutions to support innovation and mitigate financialisation. This Element shows, for example, the importance of the UK Corporate Governance Code (formerly known as the Combined Code on Corporate Governance), which in the 1990s emerged in part as a reaction to the extreme shareholder-primacy movement emanating from the United States. The Code empowers corporate executives, board directors, and public shareholders who want to shift corporate resource-allocation decisions towards innovation and away from financialisation.

In the recent experiences of AZN and GSK, we see the promise of redesigning executive pay to include explicit rewards for superior innovative performance that are not based on stock-market yields. Our analysis of the social conditions of innovative enterprise provides a rationale for UK government policy to limit the influence on corporate governance of 'predatory value extractors' (Lazonick and Shin 2020). By ensuring that the United Kingdom remains the home base of major companies in the global pharmaceutical industry, the UK government can support businesses in providing careers to teams of scientists, thus enhancing drug-development capabilities in the United Kingdom. Finally, UK government policy must address the issue of the

allocation of corporate profits to investment in innovation versus distributions
to shareholders, even if the latter only take the form of cash dividends.

3 The Innovation-Financialisation Tension in the Global Pharmaceutical Industry

The innovation process is *uncertain, collective,* and *cumulative.* Innovation
requires *strategy* to confront uncertainty by investing in the learning processes
to transform technologies and access markets in the attempt to generate
a higher-quality, lower-cost product. Innovation requires *organisation* to
engage in collective learning, which is the essence of the innovation process.
And innovation requires *finance* to sustain cumulative learning until, by transforming technologies and accessing markets, product revenues and, possibly,
profits result.

Signifying relationships and behaviour that result in productive activity, the
social conditions of innovative enterprise are *strategic control, organisational
integration,* and *financial commitment.* Strategic control endows senior executives with the power to allocate the firm's resources to particular products and
processes. The critical questions are whether those executives who exercise
strategic control have the abilities and incentives to allocate the firm's resources
to inherently uncertain innovation processes. Organisational integration mobil-
ises and incentivises the skills and efforts of people in the firm's hierarchical and
functional division of labour, its local ecosystem, and global network to engage
in collective learning (Andreoni 2018; Andreoni and Lazonick 2020). Financial
commitment provides the funding that can sustain the transformation of the
collective learning process into the cumulative learning process required to
generate, over time, a higher-quality, lower-cost product.

For an established corporation, the foundation of financial commitment is the
portion of profits that a company retains after distributing cash to shareholders
in the form of dividends and buybacks. The company can, if need be, leverage
retained profit with debt for the purpose of investing in innovation. Conversely,
a company can deplete its profits through distributions to shareholders. Indeed,
by taking on debt, selling assets, laying off employees, or drawing on cash
reserves, a company can even distribute more than 100 per cent of profits to
shareholders over a sustained period of time.

A high payout ratio – dividends plus buybacks as a percentage of profits – is
an indicator of financialisation (see Lazonick et al. 2019). But the impact of
financialisation on innovation is not simply, or even primarily, because distributions to shareholders erode financial commitment. A company that has
profited, and may continue to profit, from successful innovation undertaken in

the past often has access to accumulated financial reserves that can sustain high payout ratios for years on end (Lazonick et al. 2017).

Hence, it is possible for a cash-rich company to simultaneously, for a period of time, have both a high payout ratio and sufficient internal funds available for investment in innovation (measured in terms of R&D expenditure, for example). Our research has found, however, many cases of companies that have done large-scale buybacks over a period of years, when the cash flow is available, only to find themselves financially strapped when technological, market, or competitive conditions change (see, e.g., Carpenter and Lazonick 2017; Lazonick 2022a). It is well established, moreover, that a publicly listed company is reluctant to cut its dividends, so that, when industrial conditions reduce its cash flow, the attempt to maintain its level of dividend payments may cut into the financial resources that it has for operations.

Even when, in the presence of a high shareholder payout ratio, cash flow for reinvestment in productive capabilities remains adequate, a *more immediate* deleterious impact of financialised behaviour on the innovative capability of a once-successful company is the undermining of strategic control and organisational integration – which will eventually have a negative impact on profits. Senior executives who, with their stock-based remuneration, are incentivised to make use of their power to allocate the firm's resources to do distributions to shareholders for the sake of improving the company's stock-price performance, tend to lack the incentives to allocate the firm's resources to innovative investment strategies. Indeed, once this shift in the incentive structure occurs and these executives go down the path of financialised resource allocation, they may lose the ability, even if they once possessed it, to envision and implement the types of investments in organisational learning required for the next round of innovation. Pressure on management from shareholders to increase distributions may also undermine the social conditions of innovative enterprise.

An innovation strategy requires a firm to *retain-and-reinvest* (Lazonick 2015, 2019a): it retains profits to reinvest in employees' productive capabilities. In contrast, a financialised firm tends to engage in *downsize-and-distribute*: it lays off workers and depresses wages, outsources production, and sells off assets while using some or all of the extra cash flow to increase distributions to shareholders. As a result of downsize-and-distribute, employees are deprived of the opportunity to engage in collective and cumulative learning, and the company is deprived of the innovative products that organisational learning can generate.

In between retain-and-reinvest and downsize-and-distribute is a resource-allocation regime that we call *dominate-and-distribute*: a firm that has secured a stream of profits by establishing a dominant position in a product market – for example, a patented blockbuster pharmaceutical drug – can avoid downsizing even as it focuses on distributing these profits to shareholders. At some point, however, that dominant position may disappear. Unless the firm engages in a renewed retain-and-reinvest strategy (if it is not too late to do so), it will eventually enter the realm of downsize-and-distribute.

With financialisation undermining strategic control and organisational integration, at some point the financialised company will lack the funding to engage in financial commitment. Our research shows, however, that the injurious impacts on strategic control and organisational integration tend to be more severe when the form of distributions to shareholders consists of buybacks in addition to, or instead of, dividends. Stock buybacks done as open-market repurchases tend to reward *sharesellers* who are in the business of timing the buying and selling of shares, with insider knowledge of when open-market repurchases are actually taking place. These well-positioned sharesellers include corporate executives themselves with their stock-based pay as well as hedge-fund managers (Lazonick and Shin 2020).

In contrast, dividends provide an income stream to *shareholders* for, as the name says, holding shares. While corporations are reluctant to cut dividends even when profits decline, satisfying stable shareholders with a consistent income stream, buybacks are much more volatile, typically soaring when profits and stock prices are high and declining in downturns when profits and stock prices are depressed. All other things equal, the resource-allocation strategy of a company with a high payout ratio based on dividends will tend to be less financialised than a company with a high payout ratio based largely on buybacks. A high dividend payout ratio may constrain financial commitment, but it will tend to do less damage to strategic control and organisational integration than a high buyback payout ratio.

As we shall see in this Element, this analysis of the different impacts of dividends and buybacks on the social conditions of innovative enterprise is of prime importance for understanding the evolution of the tension between innovation and financialisation at AZN and GSK. Both companies are highly active in developing, manufacturing, and selling drugs in the United States, and hence have had exposure to the extreme adherence to the shareholder-value ideology that pervades US corporate governance.

As an indicator of the tension between innovation and financialisation, we examine relative shareholder payouts and the innovative productivity performance of the eight largest global pharmaceutical companies by revenues based in the United States and six of the eight top companies in Europe, which include the two UK-based pharmaceutical companies, AZN and GSK. (Data on innovative productivity are not available for Merck Group, based in Germany, and Novo Nordisk, based in Denmark.)

Figure 2 graphs the changing total shareholder payouts – dividends and buybacks combined – as percentages of net income (TSP) by the eight Europe-based pharmaceutical companies (EUR) and the eight US-based pharmaceutical companies (USA) that had the highest revenues in their regions in 2021. The columns in the graph break down TSP into percentages of net income in the form of cash dividends (DVP) and stock buybacks (BBP) by these eight EUR and eight USA companies for the four five-year subperiods from 2002 through

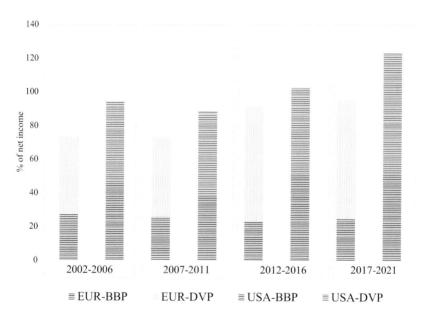

Figure 2 Percentages of net income distributed to shareholders in the form of stock buybacks (BBP) and cash dividends (DVP), 2002–21, by the eight largest Europe-based (EUR) and eight largest US-based (USA) pharmaceutical companies by revenues, 2002–21

Note: The eight largest US-based (USA) companies are ABT/ABB: Abbott Pharmaceuticals, 2002 to 2009 and AbbVie, 2010 to 2021; AMGN: Amgen; BMY: Bristol-Myers Squibb; GILD: Gilead; JNJ: Johnson and Johnson; LLY: Eli Lilly; MRK: Merck; PFE: Pfizer. The eight largest European (EUR) companies are AZN: AstraZeneca (UK); BAYN: Bayer (GER); GSK: GlaxoSmithKline (UK); NVS: Novartis (CH); ROG: Roche (CH); SAN: Sanofi (FRA); NOVO'B: Novo Nordisk (DEN); MRK. DE: Merck KGaA (GER).

Source: Authors' analysis and graphic based on S&P Capital IQ and company annual reports.

2021. In all four subperiods, both TSP and BBP were higher for the USA than for EUR companies. Although USA did relatively more buybacks than EUR, USA distributed substantial dividends in all four periods. In both EUR and USA, TSP fell in 2007–11 compared with 2002–6 because of the impact of the 2008–9 financial crisis. In the period 2012–16, BBP rose sharply in USA, while buybacks fell to their lowest proportion of net income for the four time periods in EUR. These data suggest that throughout the two decades, USA was more financialised than EUR and that after 2012 financialisation became even more extreme in USA while the opposite was the case in EUR.

By the TSP measure, USA was much more financialised than EUR throughout 2002–21, with a far higher percentage of net income being absorbed by stock buybacks. EUR TSP was by no means low, but its focus was on dividends, especially in the 2010s. USA distributions were more focused on buybacks throughout the two decades, with the predilection for buybacks increasing in the 2010s.

Among the companies that constitute EUR and USA, distributions to shareholders differed. Table 3 shows net income, dividends, and buybacks as well as TSP, DVP, and BBP for each of the EUR companies for 2002–11 and 2012–21, listed in order of net income (in US dollars) for the decade 2002–11. In the first decade, GSK had the highest net income, dividends, buybacks, and TSP of the eight companies. Its DVP was first and BBP was second to AZN.[4] In 2012–21, GSK's net income was almost $17 billion less than the previous decade, but it paid out about $9 billion more in dividends. The decline of AZN's net income from 2002–11 to 2012–21 was $15 billion greater than that of GSK's decline, but its DVP more than tripled. In the period 2012–21, GSK and AZN had by far the highest TSP of the Europe-based companies. But as their profits declined, each company reduced their buybacks significantly, both in absolute terms and as a percentage of net income.

Later in this Element, we argue that, while the high levels of DVP of AZN and GSK in 2012–21 deprived these companies of internal finance for innovation, of significance for their transitions from financialisation to innovation over the decade was the sharp shift of each UK company away from buybacks compared with the 2000s. Indeed, as we shall see, since 2013 AZN has done no

---

[4] In 2002–11, $1.6 billion of Novo Nordisk's dividends and $2.3 billion of its buybacks were payments to Novo Group, the industrial foundation that controls Novo Nordisk so that the company's external DVP was 28 per cent and external BBP was 39 per cent. In 2012–21, the external payout ratios were DVP 35 per cent and BBP 37 per cent. Both types of distributions to shareholders reduce the retained earnings available to Novo Nordisk for reinvestment as a pharmaceutical company, but only the external buybacks seek to manipulate the company's stock price.

Table 3 Net income (NI), dividends (DV), buybacks (BB), and payout ratios (TSP, DVP, BBP), by the eight largest Europe-based (EUR) and eight largest US-based (USA) pharmaceutical companies by revenues, 2002–11 and 2012–21

EUR TOP 8

Company	2002–11						2012–21					
	NI	BB	DV	BBP	DVP	TSP	NI	BB	DV	BBP	DVP	TSP
	$bn			% of NI			$bn			% of NI		
AstraZeneca	58	25	23	43	40	84	26	3	36	10	136	146
Bayer	21	–	11	0	52	52	25	–	24	0	97	97
GlaxoSmithKline	78	28	47	36	60	96	61	8	56	12	93	105
Merck KGaA	11	–	1	0	9	9	18	–	7	0	38	38
Novo Nordisk	16	8	5	54	30	84	55	25	26	45	47	92
Novartis	77	20	29	26	38	64	113	36	67	32	59	91
Roche	60	5	29	9	48	56	115	29	73	25	63	88
Sanofi	43	9	24	20	56	77	67	16	44	24	66	90

Table 3 (cont.)

USA TOP 8

Company	2002–11						2012–21					
	NI	BB	DV	BBP	DVP	TSP	NI	BB	DV	BBP	DVP	TSP
	$bn			% of NI			$bn			% of NI		
Abbott/AbbVie	37	7	20	18	54	72	57	41	40	71	69	141
Amgen	30	36	1	121	2	122	61	47	29	77	48	125
Bristol-Myers Squibb	37	2	23	5	61	66	20	19	30	96	152	248
Eli Lilly	26	1	18	4	69	74	39	17	22	43	55	98
Gilead Sciences	12	10	–	86	0	86	71	38	17	54	24	78
Johnson & Johnson	103	37	43	36	42	79	140	58	81	41	58	99
Merck & Co.	60	15	36	25	59	84	69	50	49	72	70	143
Pfizer	95	56	59	59	62	121	140	75	66	54	47	101

Source: Authors' calculations based on S&P Capital IQ and company annual reports.

buybacks, while GSK reduced its buybacks sharply in 2014 and subsequently its buybacks have been minimal or zero.

Table 3 also shows that among the USA companies, TSP ranged from 66 per cent to 122 per cent in 2002–11 and from 78 per cent to 248 per cent in 2012–21. Indeed, in the latter decade five of the eight companies had TSP of 100 per cent or more. At 78 per cent, the TSP of Gilead Sciences was the lowest in the group in the second decade, but only because its nearly six-fold increase in profits from 2002–11 to 2012–21 – inflated by price-gouging (Lazonick et al. 2017) – outstripped its dividends of $17 billion, which it only started paying in 2015, and its over four-fold increase in buybacks.

Figure 3 provides an initial indication of where twelve of these global pharmaceutical companies stood in 2011–20 in terms of the tension between innovation and financialisation. The size of the bubble measures the dollar value of buybacks that each company did over the ten-year period. The yellow bubbles represent the Europe-based pharmaceutical companies and the pink bubbles the USA companies. Note that, as mentioned previously, we lack innovative-productivity data for Germany's Merck and Denmark's Novo Nordisk, so they are not included in the analysis illustrated in Figure 3. In addition, since we lack historical pipeline data for Amgen and Gilead, only the top six USA companies are included in the analysis in Figure 3.

We caution that this comparative analysis is only a starting point for in-depth company-level studies, rooted in the theory of innovative enterprise, of the tension between innovation and financialisation. Each point on the horizontal axis in Figure 3 is a proxy for the prevalent allocative regime in a company, indicating to what extent a company is oriented towards innovation or financialisation. While point '0' (not displayed) on the horizontal axis refers to a company that has fully retained its net income (TSP = 0), point '1' on the horizontal axis refers to a company which has distributed 100 per cent of net income to shareholders in the form of buybacks and dividends. Point '2' at the far-right end of the horizontal axis refers to a situation where a company's total shareholder payout is two times greater than its net income. When the value of TSP is greater than the value of net income, buybacks and dividends tend to be financed through cash reserves, the liquidation of certain assets, laying off employees, or incurring debt.

If the TSP ratio is less than 1, it indicates that the company has retained a portion of its profits, having these funds available for the development of innovative products or rewarding employees for prior productive contributions. It is through such investments in productive capabilities that pharmaceutical companies develop innovative drugs to address unmet medical needs.

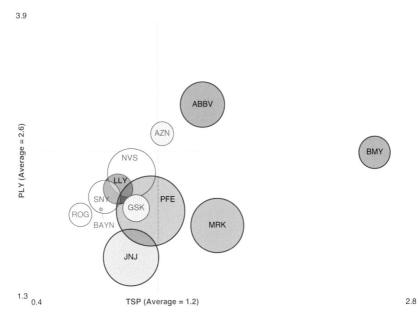

3.9

PLY (Average = 2.6)

1.3
0.4   TSP (Average = 1.2)   2.8

Figure 3 Mapping the pipeline yield (PLY) in 2021 and total shareholder payout (TSP) for six US-based and six Europe-based pharmaceutical companies, 2011–20

Note: For corporate ticker codes used in the graphic, see the note to Figure 2. PLY is the number of products under development in the pipeline as of December 2021 per billion dollars spent on R&D, 2011–20; TSP is (buybacks + dividends)/net income, 2011–20. The size of the bubbles reflects the value of buybacks done by the company, 2011–20. Yellow bubbles are Europe-based companies; pink bubbles are US-based companies.
Source: Authors' analysis and graphic based on Pharma Intelligence (Informa) Pharma R&D Annual Review 2021, S&P Capital IQ and company annual reports.

A financialised pharmaceutical company which is willing to deplete its cash through distributions to shareholders tends to downsize its productive resources in an attempt to generate even more cash to distribute to shareholders. As discussed more extensively in the case analyses of AZN and GSK, such downsizing efforts often entail reduction of the workforce and disposal of tangible and intangible assets. The key analytical challenge is to determine the effect of downsize-and-distribute on productivity through its influence on the social conditions of innovative enterprise: strategic control, organisational integration, and financial commitment.

To view the correlation between TSP and innovative productivity, each point on the vertical axis in Figure 3 refers to *pipeline yield* (PLY): the number of products under development in 2021 per $billion that each of the fourteen pharmaceutical companies spent on R&D from 2011 to 2020. We should caution that simply because a company records R&D expenditure does not necessarily mean that those expenditures will be productive. But given that the purpose of R&D is organisational learning and given that organisational learning is the essence of innovation, documentation of the relation between R&D spending and the drug pipeline is a useful preliminary metric for comparative purposes as well as for delving into the innovation processes as they occur in particular companies.

In Figure 3, any point on the vertical axis indicates a distinct productivity level in terms of PLY. In 2021, after having spent $914 billion on R&D from 2011 through 2020, the twelve pharmaceutical companies had 1,949 potential drug candidates under development, including projects in phases ranging from discovery to late-stage clinical trials. The average PLY for investments of the twelve companies was 2.6 product candidates under development. Companies in the upper section of the graph indicate levels of innovative performance above the group average, while the companies in the lower end have underperformed.

By the metrics in Figure 3, the companies located in the bottom-right corner of the box (Pfizer, Bristol-Myers Squibb, Merck) are the most highly financialised of all the companies because their PLY is below the group average while their TSP is higher than that of the companies in the group. Of the twelve companies included in the analysis, the two UK companies, AZN and GSK, have the highest PLY. At the same time, GSK has the highest TSP of the six Europe-based companies, slightly greater than that of AZN. The other European companies are all lower than GSK and AZN in terms of both TSP and PLY.

The analysis illustrated in Figure 3 does not tell us *why* these companies are distributed across the plot area based on their PLY and TSP. Because the transformation from innovation to financialisation, or vice versa, is a dynamic process that depends on the social conditions of innovative enterprise, the distribution of these companies in the plot area may vary at different points in time as the relation between innovation and financialisation changes. It is therefore necessary to analyse the companies individually to understand their changing product pipelines relative to the historical evolution of shifting resource-allocation regimes. For the purposes of this Element, Sections 4 and 5 analyse the two major UK-based competitors in the global pharmaceutical industry: AZN and GSK.

The company-level analyses explore to what extent the R&D productivity of the two UK drug companies over the past decade has provided each one with a competitive advantage over its global rivals as well as relative to each other.

Our study raises important questions about the evolving relation between resource-allocation strategies and innovative performance at each of the companies. In carrying out this empirical research, we identify the ways in which, through investment in innovation, a company accumulates productive capabilities. From this perspective, we can then seek to explain how financialisation undermines the development and utilisation of innovative capabilities within the firm.

There are a number of ways, all of them potentially complementary, by which a company can accumulate innovative capabilities. It can invest in-house, engage another company in an R&D contract or a joint venture, license another company's intellectual property, or execute an M&A deal. In-house development provides strategic managers with knowledge of the types of productive capabilities that it needs but lacks and the potential for filling that gap through collaboration, licensing, or acquisition. Indeed, without in-house development, a company will be unable to absorb the capabilities of another company or research entity with which it has partnered. Once a company has taken strategic control of productive capabilities through an acquisition, it must engage in organisational integration of those capabilities. Moreover, the company that is now exercising strategic control must make further in-house investments to generate innovative products on a sustainable basis.

At any point in time, the capabilities that a company has accumulated represent its assets. From an accounting standpoint, these assets are divided into tangibles and intangibles. Tangible assets include property, plant, equipment, and cash, while intangible assets include 'goodwill', copyrights, and patents, with the latter two representing 'intellectual property'. Goodwill is an accounting measure of the value that a company pays for an acquisition that is in excess of the 'net fair value' of the acquired assets. Goodwill looms large on the balance sheets of a company that does numerous acquisitions of other companies with organisational capabilities that the acquirer must further develop. A high valuation of goodwill may reflect market speculation in the value of acquisitions, which may turn out to be a reflection of a company's financialised strategy rather than its acquisition of innovative capability. As with any asset, tangible or intangible, whether its cost generates profits for the company of which it is now a part depends on the effectiveness of management in developing and utilising its productive capabilities to generate competitive products.

An acquisition may contribute to the innovative capabilities of the acquirer through further in-house investments. Alternatively, the acquisition may be used by the acquirer as an instrument for value extraction, and hence contribute to financialisation. An acquisition is a way for a firm to take strategic control of productive capabilities that were originally developed by another firm as a distinct unit of strategic control. In pharmaceuticals, acquisitions are often done because, for drug development that entails a new technology, a start-up has an advantage in integrating strategy and learning. Once, through investment in productive capabilities, a young company can show that it has innovative potential, it may be acquired by a more established company that wants access to that potential. Whether, subsequent to an acquisition, its assets support innovation or financialisation depends on whether the acquirer seeks to further develop the acquisition (retain-and-reinvest) or milk it for profits that can be distributed to shareholders (downsize-and-distribute).

The ideology that a company should be run to MSV lacks a theory of the business enterprise as a learning organisation (Lazonick 2022b). Legitimised by MSV ideology, financialisation essentially amounts to reneging on obligations to reward employees for their prior contributions to value creation and reducing reinvestment in organisational learning. If, as is particularly the case in the United States, senior executives who exercise strategic control increase their own stock-based remuneration through manipulative boosts in the company's stock price, they have a strong incentive to do stock buybacks as open-market repurchases (Lazonick 2014a; Lazonick and Hopkins 2016).

Stock-based pay, as it emerged in the United States in the 1980s and 1990s, reflected a shift of the business corporation from innovation to financialisation (Hopkins and Lazonick 2016). Academic proponents of MSV such as Michael Jensen and Kevin Murphy (1990) advocate using stock-based pay to align the incentives of senior executives with shareholders. The purpose of this alignment is, in Jensen's words, to 'disgorge' the 'free cash flow' from companies, based on the assumption that these executives have been simply wasting resources by investing in productive capabilities (Jensen 1986). As Jensen (1986, p. 323) puts it:

> Free cash flow is cash flow in excess of that required to fund all projects that have positive net present values when discounted at the relevant cost of capital. Conflicts of interest between shareholders and managers over payout policies are especially severe when the organization generates substantial free cash flow. The problem is how to motivate managers to disgorge the cash rather than investing it at below cost or wasting it on organization inefficiencies.

There are several problems with this statement that reflect a bias towards financialisation and the absence of an understanding of the social conditions of innovative enterprise. First, innovation is an uncertain process and hence the notion that one can calculate the 'net present value' (NPV) of an investment in innovation is absurd – which, however, has not kept it from becoming a standard 'tool' of mainstream financial economics. Students of innovation have recognised the damage that NPV measures can do when they become a basis for managerial decision-making (Baldwin and Clark 1992; Christensen, et al. 2008). Indeed, Christensen, Kaufman, and Shih label these financial tools 'innovation killers'.

Second, the definition of how much cash flow is 'free' depends on one's view of how the corporation's resources should be allocated. If one ignores the need to attract, retain, motivate, and reward large numbers of employees to engage in the organisational learning that is the essence of innovation, a substantially greater portion of cash flow can be deemed to be 'free' to be distributed to shareholders. Yet, organisational learning is the foundation of an innovative enterprise and a productive economy, all the more so in the pharmaceutical industry.

Third, the very term 'disgorge' implies that the retained earnings that a profitable company has accumulated were somehow ill-gotten, and hence it is necessary to distribute these funds to shareholders to reallocate the funds to their best alternative uses. Sustained profits are, however, the results of successful investments in organisational learning, in which the firm's employees are the prime participants. As such, they must be motivated and rewarded. Shareholders of publicly listed companies are simply households as savers, either through their direct purchases of shares on the market or indirectly through asset managers. It is business firms, not financial markets, which, by investing in productive capabilities that can generate competitive products, determine 'best alternative uses' (Lazonick and Shin 2020, ch. 7).

Since the mid-1980s, Jensenite 'agency theory' has legitimised the growing tendency in US publicly listed companies to do stock buybacks. In this looting of the US business corporation, US-based Big Pharma companies have played a leading role. For the decade 2011–20, seventeen US pharmaceutical companies in the S&P 500 Index spent $387.3 billion on buybacks and $341.8 billion on dividends. The combined distributions to shareholders of $620.8 billion represented 116 per cent of the net income of these seventeen companies over the decade and were 17.4 per cent more than the $620.8 billion that these companies spent on R&D.

As we have noted, incentivising these distributions to shareholders has been the stock-based pay of US pharmaceutical executives. Over the decade, 2010–19, total remuneration of pharmaceutical executives named in company proxy statements who were among the 500 highest-paid executives in the United States ranged from a low average of $20.7 million in 2010 (twenty-three executives), with 73 per cent stock-based, to a high average of $45.1 million in 2015 (thirty-three executives), with 88 per cent stock-based. In the United

States, the design of stock options and stock awards permits executives to realise gains from stock-price increases that result from stock-market speculation and manipulation. Stock buybacks done as open-market repurchases give US senior executives a powerful means of manipulating the stock prices of the companies that they head. By creating or accentuating upward momentum of a company's stock price, open-market repurchases in turn foment further speculative increases in the company's stock price (Lazonick et al. 2019; see also Tulum and Lazonick 2018).

As documented by Hopkins and Lazonick (2016), the use of stock options as a mode of executive remuneration in the United States from the 1950s to the 1970s did not incentivise stock buybacks because the Securities and Exchange Commission (SEC) could have charged a company that did large-scale buybacks with stock-price manipulation. The adoption of SEC Rule 10b-18 in November 1982 gave corporate executives a 'safe harbour' to do buybacks on a scale that would previously have been viewed as manipulative (Palladino 2018; Jacobson and Lazonick 2022). Jacobson and Lazonick (2022) call Rule 10b-18 a 'license to loot'.

In the United States, the explicit purpose of stock options for senior executives in the period 1950–76 was to provide the recipients with a tax dodge to avoid ordinary personal marginal tax rates that were as high as 91 per cent in the 1950s and were still at 70 per cent in 1980 by having the realised gains from stock options taxed at the much lower capital-gains tax rate (25 per cent during most of this period). To be eligible for this favourable tax treatment, an executive had to hold the shares for at least one year after exercising the option, thus risking a decline in before-tax realised gains. From the late 1950s, a political backlash occurred in the United States against this special tax treatment for corporate executives' stock-based pay, and in 1976 the US Congress abolished this tax dodge (Hopkins and Lazonick 2016).

All this changed in the 1980s with the rise of the New Economy business model, a characteristic feature of which was the use of broad-based stock-option plans to recruit large numbers of professional, technical, and administrative personnel from secure 'lifetime' employment at established Old Economy companies such as IBM, Hewlett-Packard, Motorola, Merck, Pfizer, and Johnson & Johnson, among others, to inherently insecure employment in young start-up companies whose future growth was highly uncertain (Lazonick 2009, ch. 2). During the 1980s, large numbers of relatively young employees at New Economy companies became very rich when their companies did initial public offerings (IPOs) on NASDAQ. The senior executives of established companies demanded stock-based pay, now taxed at top marginal personal rates that were as low as 28 per cent in the late 1980s, on which they would reap realised gains from stock-price movements.

Until May 1991, these senior executives, as 'insiders' had to wait six months after exercising an option before they could realise the gains for themselves. That changed in May 1991 when, after considerable lobbying by corporate executives, the SEC ruled that the six-month waiting period would begin on the grant date of the option rather than the exercise date, and since the minimum period for an option to vest after a grant is one year, the executives were now permitted to realise the gains on the options immediately upon exercise. This rule change in turn enabled senior executives to coordinate option exercises with stock buyback activity, the execution of which they controlled.

Our analysis of the changing balance between innovation and financialisation at AZN and GSK, therefore, pays close attention to value extraction as dividends versus value extraction as buybacks as well as to the stock-based components of total CEO remuneration. Currently, at major UK corporations, the CEO remuneration scheme includes many different components of pay including salary, bonus, pension, stock options, and stock awards. Figure 4 shows the components of CEO pay averaged across the same seventy-two large UK companies for the fiscal years 2000, 2007, 2015, 2016, and 2017. Total

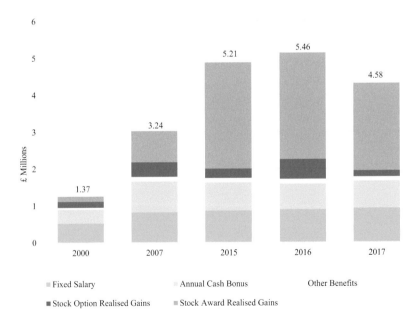

Figure 4 Salary, bonus, stock options, and other components of CEO total remuneration (£ million), seventy-two UK companies, 2000, 2007, 2015, 2016, and 2017

Source: Authors' analysis and graphic based on company annual reports.

compensation averaged £1.37 million in 2000 and was as high as (for the years for which we collected the data) £5.46 million in 2016.

Figure 5 transforms these data into percentages of total remuneration that are cash-based and stock-based. In 2000, the stock-based portion of CEO pay averaged 24 per cent but was as high as 66 per cent in 2016. In all five years, the higher the percentage of compensation that was stock-based, the higher the total average CEO remuneration.

Ostensibly, the various components of CEO pay and their specific conditions for realising gains reflect attempts by the board's remuneration committee to attract, retain, motivate, and reward the CEO for doing her job of investing in the productive capabilities of the company to generate competitive products. Whether the components of pay, and particularly those that are stock-based, perform this function is, however, a question that requires both close scrutiny of the schemes implemented by the company concerned – in this study AZN and GSK – and the institutional environment in the nation in which it is headquartered.

At the national institutional level, the extent to which senior corporate executives should be able to realise gains on stock-based pay has received far more discussion in the United Kingdom than in the United States. As recognised

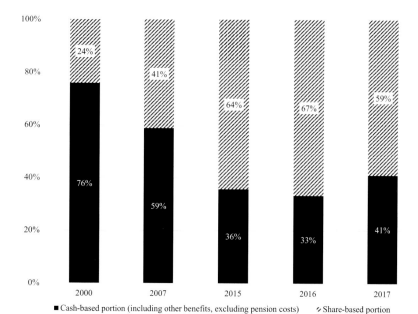

Figure 5 Proportions of cash-based and share-based components of CEO total remuneration, seventy-two UK companies, 2000, 2007, 2015, 2016, and 2017
Source: Authors' analysis and graphic based on company annual reports.

by the Greenbury Report (1995, p. 10), issued by a committee of the UK Confederation of British Industry in 1995:

> We also believe there to be a key issue about performance which has received too little attention in the public discussion. The UK's industrial performance has greatly improved in recent years. It is vital that this improvement should continue. But the performance of our companies depends to an important extent on the Directors and senior executives who lead them. The remuneration packages UK companies offer must, therefore, be sufficient to attract, retain and motivate Directors and managers of the highest quality.

By the early 1990s, as documented in the book, *In Search of Excess: The Overcompensation of American Executive*s (1991), the prominent compensation consultant Graef S. Crystal sketched out what is called the 'ratchet job' for boosting average CEO pay over time (Murphy 1999; Lazonick 2014b). Using corporate funds, the CEO of a US business corporation hires a compensation consultant to recommend a remuneration package to the board's compensation committee. The consultant's report benchmarks other corporate CEOs and tends to place the CEOs who have hired the consultant in the 75th percentile in terms of performance and, hence, pay. CEOs of other companies dominate the board's compensation committee, and this process of ratcheting up CEO pay is in their own personal interest. Moreover, with the realised gains from stock-based pay becoming an increasing portion of total remuneration, sharp increases in CEO pay in stock-market booms set new norms for total CEO remuneration. When the stock-market declines and, with it, CEO pay, the compensation committee recommends that the CEO should be granted more stock options, which are now at low exercise prices, and/or stock awards, with an MSV mandate to do whatever it takes to boost the company's stock prices, at which point stock buybacks greatly augment the power of the remuneration ratchet.

By the mid-1990s, this detachment of US-style CEO pay from the productive performance of a company was apparent to the UK Confederation of British Industry in its promulgation of the Greenbury Report, which focused on executive remuneration in articulating its 'code of best practice'. The Greenbury Report emphasised structuring the remuneration packages of UK managers and directors to incentivise them to focus on improvements in industrial performance – that is, value creation – rather than the value extraction incentivised by US-style stock-based pay. As we will see in Sections 4 and 5, the changing modes of CEO remuneration at AZN and GSK can be understood as integral to the changing tension between innovation and financialisation within the company. Specifically, the more US-style stock-based pay has been prevalent in the remuneration packages of the CEOs, the more financialised the company, whereas restrictions on CEO stock-based pay to conform with a UK-style 'code of good practice' have reflected an attempt by the board to move the corporate orientation away from financialisation towards innovation.

4 AstraZeneca

4.1 Strategy and Learning

In the 1990s, global pharmaceutical companies began to develop highly sophisticated drugs, using new scientific insights from molecular biology, including cutting-edge recombinant DNA (rDNA) technologies. Developed by young biotechnology companies in collaboration with leading scientists, these novel biologics were the products of prolonged learning efforts, invariably rooted in government-funded projects. As new drugs entered the global market, major producers of traditional pharmaceuticals strategised how to transition into this booming segment.

Zeneca PLC was incorporated as an independent pharmaceutical company in 1993 following the demerger of Imperial Chemical Industries (ICI) and the spinoff of the company's pharmaceutical division. Changing conditions of global drug markets and biomedical technologies posed a challenge to the demerged company's top executives, as they sought new ways to boost its innovative productivity. Given the scale of, and the risk associated with, the investment necessary to expand into the biologics market, many established companies chose to enter into mergers.

In the late 1990s, Zeneca embarked upon discussions with Astra AB, based in Sweden. The senior executives of both companies were aware that neither Astra nor Zeneca possessed the productive capabilities necessary to transition into biologics. Both companies were searching for the ideal partner with which to pursue a merger-of-equals before becoming a takeover target amidst rising consolidation in the global pharmaceutical industry. Their merger into AZN in late 1999 created the world's fourth-largest pharmaceutical company and the UK's fifth-largest industrial organisation (see Figure 6).

Investor AB played a key role in the merger and further development of AZN. Founded in 1916, Investor is a Swedish investment company that has been tightly controlled by the country's most influential industrialists, the Wallenberg family, through a governance mode known in the Nordic countries as the industrial foundation. Strategic control within industrial foundations has tended to be secured through a dual-class share structure. In the early 1920s, Astra, which had been founded as a Swedish pharmaceutical company in 1913 but was nationalised in 1920 after its bankruptcy, was acquired from the Swedish government by a consortium of Swedish industrialists and bankers, including Jacob Wallenberg. Subsequently, Investor held a controlling interest in Astra through

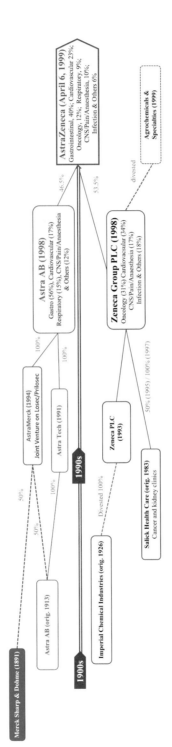

Figure 6 Pre-merger evolution of AZN

Source: Authors' own illustration based on the compilation of information from various sources.

a dual-class share structure, and at the end of 1998, preceding the merger with Zeneca, was still the pharmaceutical company's most influential shareholder.

Over the past two decades, Investor has been a significant shareholder in other global companies, based in Sweden and abroad. However, prior to the merger, Astra was the largest holding in Investor's investment portfolio. Reflecting the family's 'buy-to-build' philosophy, Investor's business strategy entails a long-term investment horizon with no timeline to exit. Investor favours involvement in companies with a dual-class share structure, which enables it to have active representation on corporate boards, with two or more directors including the board chairman.

Following the merger, AZN's newly issued ordinary shares with one class of voting and dividend rights replaced the voting and non-voting shares of Astra, bringing the company's dual-class share structure to an end. In AZN's new single-class share structure, the majority of shares were owned by the former Zeneca shareholders. Following the merger, however, the Wallenberg family managed to acquire significant board representation, with former Astra executives filling seven of fourteen director seats. AZN's board chairman was Percy Barnevik, CEO of the Swiss-Swedish power company ABB, in which Investor was the largest shareholder. He was also non-executive chairman of Investor. Marcus Wallenberg, CEO of Investor, was a director of AZN. Other former Astra executives became AZN's non-executive chairman, executive deputy chairman, executive director of R&D, chair of the remuneration committee, and executive director of business development.

During the first five-year period following the merger, the directors with strong ties to the Wallenberg family were involved in major strategic decisions. During 2004, a series of events unfolded that reduced Investor's influence on AZN's board. It began with the pivotal ruling by the European Commission that required Volvo to sell its stake in Scania. With major stakes in both AZN and Scania, Investor reduced its shareholding in AZN from 5.0 per cent to 3.75 per cent to raise nearly $1 billion to purchase the vote-heavy A-shares of Scania (Brown-Humes 2004).

Investor's downsizing of its shareholding in AZN resulted in a major transformation of the company's board and senior executive team in 2004 and 2005. Barnevik, who had resigned from his chairmanship of Investor in 2002 in the wake of a scandal concerning the pension he had been awarded when he had retired as CEO of ABB (Woodruff 2002), stepped down from his post as AZN chairman in 2004. He was replaced by Louis Schweitzer, former chairman of French automobile maker Renault, who had no prior ties to Investor. In 2005, Schweitzer removed AZN's first CEO, Thomas McKillop, filling the position with the head of the company's US operations, David Brennan.

Although Brennan was not the frontrunner among candidates to replace McKillop, the board promoted him from president of the company's North American operations to lead AZN's global operations as the new CEO.

During Schweitzer's tenure, the AZN board continued to undergo major transformation, in part to address a movement that had been occurring since the 1990s within the UK business community to increase the number of independent directors of UK companies. Prior to Schweitzer's arrival, major plans to amend the company's corporate-governance policies were underway, including the appointment in 2003 of Michele Hooper, a corporate-governance expert, as an independent director.

AZN's status as the world's fourth largest pharmaceutical company following the merger was based largely on sales of the company's flagship ulcer drug Losec/Prilosec and blood-pressure drug Zestril. AZN generated a steady flow of revenues from these drugs, which accounted for nearly 50 per cent of the company's total revenues. With both drugs set to lose patent protection in major markets over the next few years, however, AZN struggled to come up with new replacements.

Given the prospective reduction of revenues because of patent expiry, AZN under McKillop responded by modestly increasing its R&D expenditure in the hope of developing drug replacements (see Figure 7). A successful replacement for the company's ulcer drug arrived in 2001 with the approval of Nexium, a slightly more advanced version of Losec/Prilosec that had been developed by Astra researchers in the 1990s. The launch of Nexium was followed by Seroquel, a controversial anti-psychotic drug developed in the 1980s in the United States by scientists at Zeneca's Wilmington, Delaware R&D facility (Griffiths 1996). AZN also found success with Crestor, a cholesterol-lowering drug. In the decade following the merger, booming sales of Seroquel along with Nexium and Crestor enabled AZN to more than double its annual product revenues from $15.1 billion in 1999 to $31.6 billion in 2008.

Brennan became CEO at the onset of a period of rapid growth of the company between 2004 and 2007, with an average annual growth of product sales of 12.25 per cent. In the following four-year period (2008–11), however, the company's product sales only grew at an annual average of 3.25 per cent. By the end of his tenure as CEO in 2012, Brennan had initiated a major R&D overhaul as several more AZN products faced patent expiry. A major increase in R&D employment related to globalisation of the labour force occurred from 2010 to 2012, with total R&D employment rising from 12,000 to 15,700 (see Figure 8). This expansion in R&D employment was followed by a deep restructuring with large scale job cuts in high-income regions, which left AZN with 11,300 R&D employees in 2011.

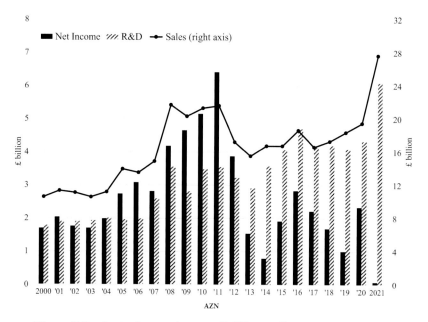

Figure 7 Product sales, net income, R&D spending at AZN, 2000–21

Note: The net income for AZN in 2021 reflects the extraordinary expenses the company accrued during the year.

Source: Authors' analysis and graphic based on S&P Capital IQ and company annual reports.

Replacing Brennan as AZN's CEO was Pascal Soriot, who had to cope with the company's plummeting sales, which dropped from $33.6 billion in 2011 to $22.1 billion in 2018, largely as a result of patent expiry of AZN's flagship products. Under Soriot, who in 2022 remains AZN's CEO, there has been steady sales growth of respiratory products. But his main focus has been a major reorganisation of the company to support biopharma product innovation. The transformation has centred on the combination of R&D units in six therapy areas – respiratory/inflammation, cardiovascular, gastrointestinal, neuroscience, oncology, and infection – into three focused R&D units: BioPharmaceuticals, Oncology, and Rare Diseases following the acquisition of Alexion. With the introduction of COVID-19 vaccines and therapies, AZN created a separate Vaccines and Immune Therapies Unit in 2022.

In reorienting the company to grow through internal innovation, Soriot has built on his experience at Roche's wholly owned US subsidiary Genentech, where he oversaw the integration of Genentech and Roche R&D operations. AZN's shift to biologics through a series of acquisitions has enabled the company to boost its clinical pipeline and alleviate concerns over AZN's diminishing R&D productivity.

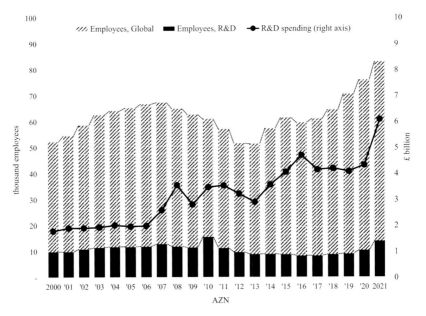

Figure 8 R&D spending (in £ billion), global employees and R&D employees
at AZN, 2000–21

Source: Authors' analysis and graphic based on company annual reports.

Figure 9 provides data for selected years on the evolution of the pipeline of
AZN by different phases in the drug discovery process, as discussed in
Section 2. We can observe a cyclical variation reflecting the drugs moving
along the different phases of drug discovery, as well as a steady increase in the
number of drugs that have been launched. There is no direct relation, however,
between these dynamics in the drugs pipeline and variation in pharma product
revenues. More importantly, these data do not allow us to understand changes in
the organisational learning process within AZN under, first, Brennan, and, then,
Soriot. Fortunately, this process was documented for AZN by its scientists in
two studies published in 2014 and 2018, covering the periods 2005–10 and
2012–16, respectively.

In the first study, published in *Nature Reviews,* Cook et al. (2014) explain
how the decline of the company's R&D productivity between 2005 and 2010
resulted from a shift in the organisational culture during the 2000s away
from incentivising 'truth-seeking' efforts to learn more about diseases and
towards rewarding 'progression-driven' behaviours to meet 'numerical volume-based goals'. Cook et al. blamed the 'industrialization of R&D' at AZN
for the company's clinical failures. The industrialisation of R&D, they
argued, encouraged the adoption of a 'volume-based approach' that stressed

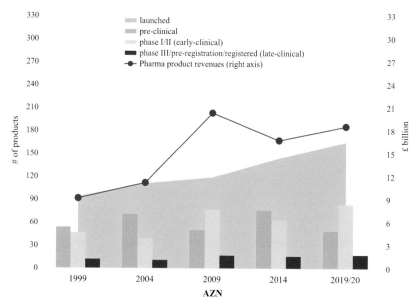

Figure 9 AZN's pharmaceutical products sales (£ billion), number of products launched and under development (pre-, early-, and late-clinical stages), 1999-FY2019/3Q2020

Note: The data for pipeline (preclinical, early-clinical, and late-clinical) and launched products illustrated in the figure are cumulative totals of product development activities reported by the company in the respective year. The latest available data for annual pharma product revenue is 2019. The latest cumulative totals include products that were under development (pipeline) or launched in 2019 through the third quarter of 2020. **Source:** Authors' analysis and graphic based on Pharmaprojects.

the 'use of quantity-based metrics to drive productivity', but which ultimately undermined the 'quality and sustainability' of product pipelines (p. 419).

The scientists described the reorganisation of R&D, begun towards the end of Brennan's tenure, to implement a new 'five-dimensional framework' (Cook et al. 2014), which features decision-making guidelines for R&D teams to improve AZN's innovative productivity. It was the presence of these forward-looking scientists at AZN that made it logical for the board to appoint the like-minded Soriot as the new CEO in 2013. Under Soriot, these dissidents to the 'volume-based approach' have gained more power within the R&D organisation. Rather than further expanding the company's clinical pipeline, AZN has focused on enhancing the productivity of existing capabilities to improve the yield of the company's drug development efforts.

These learning processes helped the R&D organisation reduce the attrition rate of the company's clinical candidates and increase the success rate of late-stage trials while enhancing the efficiency of the company's overall R&D spending. In 2018, seventeen senior R&D managers at AZN, including three of the authors of the 2014 *Nature Reviews* article, one of whom was the current executive vice-president of biopharmaceutical R&D, Menelas Pangalos, wrote a follow-up piece in which they examined the progress of clinical candidates in the company's product pipeline between 2012 and 2016 (Morgan et al. 2018). In addition to narrowing the company's research focus to fewer disease areas and particular classes of targets, AZN established a thorough internal screening process to carefully evaluate and select fewer lead compounds to be further evaluated during the preclinical studies for their safety and efficacy. This reduction in the number of strategically selected and thoroughly assessed lead compounds to be pursued is responsible for the major improvement that AZN has achieved in the productivity of R&D, which became superior to the industry average in every stage of the drug discovery and development process.

This decision-making framework developed by AZN has encouraged project teams to assess the validity of targets by utilising new scientific knowledge developed through exploring disease genomics and has prevented the R&D organisation from pursuing those lead compounds for which insights into disease biology are limited. The drug-development efforts on genetically valid-ated targets began to improve the company's R&D yield in terms of drug candidates that successfully progressed through clinical trials. This innovative transformation of AZN's R&D has enhanced the company's internal capabil-ities for collaborative learning with the world's leading genomics research institutes for the purpose of gaining insights into the pathology of various complex diseases. At the same time, the company's advances in organisational learning have augmented its capabilities for integrating innovative acquisitions into its organisation.

4.2 Innovation through In-House Development and Acquisition

In addition to in-house drug development, AZN's growth has been highly dependent on acquiring other companies and integrating them into its organisa-tional-learning process. Over time AZN also restructured its product portfolio in part by divesting certain assets and units. Table 4 shows AZN's acquisitions, major licensing deals, and divestments from 2001 to 2021.

McKillop, AZN CEO from the merger in 2000 to the end of 2005, focused on improving the company's financial performance. During his tenure, AZN did no

Table 4 Selected acquisitions, licensing, and divestments at AZN, 2001–21

			AZN Selected M&A (deals for value disclosed)		
				Total Value (£ million)	
CEO	Year	Acquisition target/acquirer	Acquired	Divested	Capabilities acquired/ divested
Thomas McKillop	**2001**	Penicillin/other injectables mfg. sites, anaesthetics units		136	
	2002	Sular product line by First Horizon		122	Anti-hypertensive drug line
	2003	Durscan & Marlow Food		70	
		Abgenix [products licensed-in/acquired minority]	n.d.		Oncology
	2004	NLA Holding by Syngenta		267	Advanta seed business
		Array [product licensed-in]	n.d.		Oncology
		Cambridge Antibody Tech [acquired 20% equity]	75		Immuno-oncology
	2005	Protherics [products licensed-in/acquired minority]	n.d.		Anti-infectives
		Targacept [product licensed-in]	n.d.		Neuroscience
		Astex [product licensed-in]	n.d.		Oncology
		AtheroGenics [product licensed-in/acquired minority]	75		Cardiovascular

Table 4 (cont.)

		AZN Selected M&A (deals for value disclosed)			
			Total Value (£ million)		Capabilities acquired/ divested
CEO	Year	Acquisition target/acquirer	Acquired	Divested	
David Brennan	**2006**	Anaesthetics/analgesic business/others		203	
		Cambridge Antibody Technology [acquired 80% equity]	567		Oncology
	2007	KuDOS Pharma [fully acquired]	120		Oncology
		Arrow Therapeutics [fully acquired]	77		Anti-infectives
		MedImmune [fully acquired]	7,702		Immuno-oncology
	2008	TIKA (OTC unit) by GSK; sixteen prescription drugs		192	
	2010	Rigel Pharma [fully acquired]	793		Autoimmune disease
		Novexel Corp. [fully acquired]	231		Anti-infectives
	2011	Astra Tech AB by Dentsply		1,207	Dental
	2012	Nexium brand by Pfizer		159	OTC
		Ardea [fully acquired]	636		Autoimmune disease
		Amylin Pharma [co-acquired with BristolMyersSquibb]	4,481		Diabetes
		Link Medicine Corp. [neuroscience assets only]	n.d.		Neuroscience
Pascal Soriot	**2013**	FibroGen [for roxadustat product line]	n.d.		Urology/anaemia
		Spirogen [fully acquired]	276		Urology/anaemia
		Pearl Therapeutics [fully acquired]	751		Respiratory

Year	Deal	Value	Therapy area
2014	Omthera [fully acquired]	250	Cardiovascular
	Amplimmune [fully acquired]	309	Cardiovascular
	Moderna Therapeutics [partial equity]	286	Oncology
	Definiens AG [fully acquired]	119	Oncology diagnostics
	Almirall [respiratory product assets only]	1,312	Respiratory
	BMS' shares in the JV to fully own Amylin	2,631	Diabetes
2015	Myalept (metreleptin for injection) by Aegerion Pharma	205	Autoimmune (rare) diseases
	Durvalumab co-commercialisation by Celgene	306	Oncology
	Entasis [spinoff]	n.d.	AZN anti-infectives unit
	Caprelsa (vandetanib) by Genzyme	193	Oncology (orphan indications)
2016	ZS Pharma [fully acquired]	1,793	Cardiovascular & urology
	Actavis [respiratory product assets only]	1,803	Respiratory
	Heptares Therapeutics [licensing-in]	329	Immuno-oncology
	Entocort by Perrigo's Elan Pharma unit	250	Gastroenterology
	AZD4901 by Millendo [licensed-out/acquired minority]	151	Endocrine diseases
	Anti-infective products portfolio by Pfizer	1,190	Small-molecule anti-infectives
	AZD7986 by Insmed	151	COPD drug candidate
	Acerta Pharma [fully acquired]	2,774	Oncology

Table 4 (cont.)

AZN Selected M&A (deals for value disclosed)

| CEO | Year | Acquisition target/acquirer | Total Value (£ million) | | Capabilities acquired/ divested |
			Acquired	Divested	
		Moderna Therapeutics [minority]	108		Oncology
		Takeda [respiratory product assets only]	392		Respiratory
	2017	MEDI8897 by Sanofi		99	Infectious disease
		Zoladex by TerSera		205	Oncology
		Lynparza by Merck, Sharp & Dohme [co-commercialise]		1,229	Oncology
		Anaesthetic portfolio by Aspen		217	Anaesthetic
		AZD9668 by Mereo Biopharma [licensed-out /minority]	n.d.		Respiratory
	2018	Seroquel/XR commercial rights by Luye Pharma		390	Neuroscience
		Atacand commercial rights by Cheplapharm		156	Heart failure & blood pressure
		Nexium/Vimovo commercial rights by Grünenthal		535	Gastrointestinal
		Alvesco/Omnaris/Zetonna by Covis Pharma		211	Respiratory/allergy
		Viela Bio [spinoff via IPO]		181	AZN autoimmune R&D unit
	2019	ADC Therapeutics [partial equity]	n.d.		Oncology
		Innate Pharma [licensing-in]	290		Oncology
		Synagis by Sobi [US rights/minority]		1,162	Infectious disease
		Losec global rights by Cheplapharm		198	Gastrointestinal
		Arimidex/Casodex commercial rights by Juvisé		140	Oncology

Year	Transaction			
	Seroquel/XR commercial rights by Cheplapharm		165	Neuroscience
	Daiichi Sankyo [co-development of Enhertu]	5,300		Oncology
2020	Zestril/Inderal/Tenormin by Atnahs		273	Heart failure & blood pressure
	Atacand/Atacand Plus product line by Cheplapharm		309	Heart failure & blood pressure
	FDA Priority Review Voucher by Incyte Corp.		93	Rare
	Alexion [fully acquired]	30,995		Immunology (rare)
2021	Viela Bio by Horizon Therapeutics [minority]		571	AZN autoimmune R&D unit
	Crestor commercial rights by Grünenthal		230	cholesterol
	Moderna [minority]		720	mRNA
	Caelum Biosciences [controlling stake]	258		Immunology (rare)
2001–21	Other divestitures		6,192	
	Total from selected acquisitions/divestitures 2001–21	**64,733**	**18,078**	

Source: Authors' own table based on information compiled from various sources.

acquisitions. The company made some attempts at collaborative research and licensing arrangements with a small number of biotech start-ups in the United States such as Abgenix and Array BioPharma, but these engagements yielded no significant innovative outcomes.

Under McKillop, AZN shifted attention to the greater biotech community and revamped the company's licensing efforts to expand its product portfolio in oncology, neurodegenerative, cardiovascular, and anti-infectives. In 2005, the company launched a new strategy to increase its innovative productivity and grow its revenues inorganically through pursuing licensing deals with companies such as Cambridge Antibody Technology (CAT), Astex Therapeutics, and Protherics in the United Kingdom as well as Targacept and AtheroGenics in the United States. AZN's total cost of these deals included a $560-million payment to be made upfront plus $2.2 billion for contingent payments to be paid upon the products that were subject to licensing agreements achieving various clinical, regulatory, and commercial milestones.

Brennan changed direction by initiating the company's acquisition spree, starting with the most promising British companies pioneering in the field of immunotherapy drugs such as KuDOS Pharma, CAT, and Arrow Therapeutics. In 2007, AZN made its most important acquisition by taking control of the US-based immunotherapy company MedImmune. As a result, there were sharp increases in goodwill, other intangible assets, and debt on AZN's balance sheet (see Figure 10). The contributions of these acquisitions to the company's drug-innovation processes depended on (a) the nature and the extent of new productive capabilities absorbed through these acquisitions and (b) the integration of these productive capabilities into AZN's learning processes.

In 2007, Brennan completed AZN's largest acquisition, MedImmune, for $15.6 billion. Many shareholders criticised Schweitzer and Brennan for paying an excessive premium for MedImmune (Barriaux 2007; Pollack 2007). AZN's top leadership pursued the Medimmune acquisition because of the gloomy prospects for the company's R&D productivity following the failure of multiple late-stage clinical candidates reported in 2006. As cancer immunotherapies entered the market for oncology drugs in the early 2000s, Big Pharma companies, including AZN and GSK, had very limited internal capabilities to develop immunotherapies. AZN paid a high acquisition price because of intense competition to acquire a company such as MedImmune, as did other companies for similar acquisitions. For example, in April 2008, Japan's Takeda paid $8.8 billion for Millennium Pharmaceuticals, and in July 2008 Roche paid an enormous $44 billion to acquire the remaining 44 per cent stake of Genentech that the company did not yet own (the deal was completed in March 2009). Having won a bidding war against Bristol-Myers Squibb (BMS), Eli Lilly

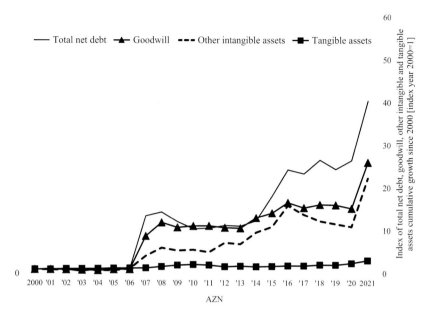

Figure 10 Intangible and tangible assets in relation to total net debt at AZN, 2000–21

Source: Authors' analysis and graphic based on S&P Capital IQ and company annual reports.

managed to complete the acquisition of ImClone Systems for $6.5 billion in October 2008. In July 2009, BMS paid $2.4 billion to acquire Medarex, a major competitor of Abgenix and CAT in the development of human antibodies.

In the cases of MedImmune and ImClone, the high prices paid for these acquisitions were in part because of the control that hedge-fund activist Carl Icahn had gained over the targets by winning major proxy fights. With AZN paying a 21 per cent premium for the shares of MedImmune and Eli Lilly a 51 per cent premium for the shares of ImClone, Icahn was able to double his money very quickly (Hamilton 2007; Saul and Pollack 2008).

Since the acquisition of MedImmune in 2007, AZN has addressed a sharp decline in the company's cash flow from operating activities through the disposal of several assets (see Table 4). In 2011, the company sold Astra Tech, its Swedish dental implants and devices subsidiary, for $1.8 billion. The following year, AZN disposed of Aptium Oncology, a subsidiary that provided outpatient oncology management and consulting services in the United States. In 2010, AZN paid $500 million for Novexel (which had been spun off from Sanofi-Aventis) to boost the company's anti-infectives franchise with a new generation of antibiotics. But in 2012, AZN divested several antimalarial brands in this therapeutic segment.

Following this restructuring, AZN's cash flow declined sharply because the new revenues that the acquisitions generated did not offset the haemor-rhaging sales of the major products in its pre-acquisition portfolio, which, as we have seen, began to fall off the patent cliff towards the end of Brennan's tenure. In addition, in 2012, several promising mid- and late-stage clinical candidates in AZN's pipeline experienced major setbacks. In response, institutional shareholders led by Neil Woodford, who was at the time a prominent asset manager at Invesco, began to pressure the AZN board to search for a replacement for Brennan. Woodford, who in 2012 had been managing Invesco's equity portfolio for over two decades, had allocated £1.64 billion to the purchase of AZN shares, 8.17 per cent of his assets under management.

When Soriot joined AZN as CEO in 2013, the company was already grappling with the problem of its ailing R&D productivity. One move was to recruit Pangalos, who had been vice-president of neuroscience at Wyeth and had become a Pfizer senior vice-president when it acquired Wyeth in 2008. Pangalos joined AZN in 2010 to lead the company's innovative medicines and early clinical development (IMED) unit. Soriot came to rely heavily on Pangalos' leadership in creating a more innovative learning culture in AZN R&D.

Working with Pangalos on the R&D leadership team were Bahija Jallal and Sean Bohen. France-educated biologist Jallal had joined MedImmune as vice-president of translation sciences in 2006, nearly a year before the acquisition of the Maryland-based company by AZN. With Soriot at the helm, Jallal was promoted from executive vice-president of R&D to president of MedImmune and executive vice-president of AZN. Under Jallal, the MedImmune unit became AZN's global hub for biologics R&D, overseeing the company's entire biologics pipeline.

In 2015, Bohen became executive vice-president of global medicines devel-opment and chief medical officer. Like Soriot, Bohen joined AZN from Genentech. When Soriot had led Roche's efforts to transform Genentech's R&D operations to become the Swiss company's new Genentech Research and Early Development (gRED) division, Bohen had served as senior vice-president responsible for early development activities at gRED.

Under this trio, AZN R&D began to engage in new learning, primarily with the objective of gaining more insight into the biology and mechanisms of diseases for which the company sought to develop new innovative treatments. Over time the focus of the company's product strategy has narrowed down to three main therapy areas: oncology; cardiovascular, renal, and metabolism (CRM); and respiratory diseases. Soriot identified immuno-oncology as the most strategic market in which AZN needed to grow. He recruited José

Baselga, the top physician at New York's Memorial Sloan Kettering Cancer Center – the world's oldest and largest institute for cancer research – to be AZN's executive vice-president, oncology R&D. Also, in 2019, Soriot promoted Pangalos to executive vice-president, biopharmaceutical R&D, which includes both CRM and respiratory diseases.

Under Soriot, AZN has consolidated its global R&D operations at three main geographic sites. The first is the newly constructed corporate headquarters located in Cambridge, UK, which became the company's main location for oncology R&D, while also consolidating most of its small-molecule and biologics R&D sites that had been scattered across the United Kingdom. After delays, this facility opened in 2019, and is, in 2022, still in the process of being made fully operational. The second main R&D site is the global hub for biologics R&D in Gaithersburg, Maryland, USA, where MedImmune's global headquarters had been located prior to its acquisition by AZN. The third major R&D hub is in Gothenburg, Sweden, continuing the legacy of AZN's predecessor, Astra, which is now supporting the entire life cycle of medicines in the global product portfolio.

Since Soriot arrived, the transformations in both the composition and age of AZN's product portfolio have been dramatic. The percentage share of oncology in total product revenues increased from 12 per cent in 2013 to 36 per cent in 2021. AZN's oncology product sales more than tripled from $4.0 billion in 2017 to $13.1 billion in 2021. AZN's total product sales increased by 81 per cent, from $20.2 billion in 2017 to $36.5 billion in 2021. This sales growth occurred even with sharp revenue declines in the company's legacy flagship products, Nexium, Synagis, and Seroquel. These products, along with others that had been losing patent protection, accounted for 35 per cent of product sales in 2013 but only 11 per cent in 2019. Despite an $8.6 billion sales drop in legacy products and CRM segments since 2013, excluding the sales of Alexion products and COVID-19 medicines, AZN's total product revenues were $3.8 billion more in 2021 than in 2013. The company's commitment to new learning in oncology began to pay off in a number of new product launches.

In 2015, the company spun off its anti-infectives unit as a standalone company. And in 2016, it sold its small-molecule assets to Pfizer. As shown in Table 4, AZN under Soriot has pursued acquisitions to support the company's internal drug development efforts. As previously discussed, oncology products' sales have been driving AZN's revenue growth with the two cancer drugs, Lynparza and Tagrisso, accounting for over half of the entire oncology segment revenues.

To clinch its prominence in the oncology market, AZN has been pursuing growing numbers of strategic partnerships for research, development, and commercialisation of drug candidates. It has been acquiring equity stakes in biopharma companies with highly anticipated oncology pipelines such as the US-based Moderna Therapeutics, which in 2020 developed a COVID-19 vaccine, and Innate Pharma, based in the Netherlands and the United States, with deal sizes ranging from $100 million to $300 million. A notable partnership into which AZN has entered is the development and commercialisation of Japan-based Daiichi Sankyo's trastuzumab deruxtecan (Enhertu), a highly effective cancer therapy that has been undergoing late-stage clinical trials. Sankyo's novel cancer therapy was granted Breakthrough Therapy Designation by the US Food and Drug Administration (FDA) for the treatment of patients with HER2-positive breast and gastric cancers.

Given the efficacy shown during clinical trials, Sankyo's cancer therapy received final regulatory approval from the FDA in December 2019. In exchange for commercialising Sankyo's cancer drug jointly, AZN paid the Japanese drug company $1.35 billion in cash up front in addition to $5.55 billion in future payments, contingent upon the drug meeting certain regulatory and performance targets. AZN decided to raise the cash to secure the deal with Sankyo by issuing new shares rather than take on additional debt that could threaten its credit rating.

In December 2020, AZN announced the acquisition of US-based Alexion Pharmaceuticals, its largest acquisition ever. When the deal closed in July 2021, it was valued at $41.1 billion, of which one-third was cash and two-thirds AZN stock. In doing the acquisition, AZN issued long-term debt of $8.0 billion and short-term debt of $4.0 billion. AZN also paid $2.3 billion debt acquired with Alexion shortly after the completion of the acquisition in 2021 (see Figure 10).

As in the case of MedImmune in 2007, the opportunity to acquire Alexion occurred because a US-based hedge fund – in this case Elliott Management – purchased Alexion shares and then sought to realise financial gains through the sale of the company to a Big Pharma corporation at a premium price (De La Merced 2017). Initially, after Elliott acquired Alexion's shares in April 2017, the pharmaceutical company rejected the proposal to sell itself. From January 2018, however, after Paul Singer of Elliott had negotiated placing his 'own' representative on Alexion's board, the proposal for a sale of the company gained more traction. Negotiating the sale to AZN was its former CEO David Brennan, who had been a director of Alexion since 2014 and chairman since 2017. With the acquisition of Alexion, AZN secured a company which had revenues of $6.1 billion in 2020, including its two blockbuster drugs, Soliris with sales of $4.1 billion and Ultomiris $1.1 billion.

Although the opportunity to buy Alexion could not have been foreseen when Soriot became CEO of AZN in 2012, the acquisition helped AZN achieve revenues of $37.4 billion in 2021, bringing AZN much closer to Soriot's revenue goal of $40 billion by 2023. With the acquisition, AZN's stock price continued to soar, but the benefits that AZN will derive from Alexion depend on how it invests profits from both its patented drugs and, prospectively, successful drugs from those now in its pipeline. To better integrate Alexion, AZN has set up its global R&D headquarters for rare diseases at Alexion's base in Cambridge, Massachusetts.

4.3 Distributions to Shareholders

As we outlined in Section 3, dividends provide an income stream to all shareholders for holding shares, whereas stock buybacks done as open-market repurchases reward those sharesellers who are in the business of timing their stock trades. These types of stock buybacks are nothing more than (currently legal) tools to manipulate the company's stock price, and thus manifest the financialised firm. Our analysis of the changing balance between innovation and financialisation at AZN (and in the next section of this Element, GSK), therefore, pays close attention to value extraction as dividends versus value extraction as buybacks. AZN paid out cash in the form of both dividends and buybacks in the first decade of the century and into the second decade. Since 2013, however, the first full year that Soriot was CEO, AZN has ceased doing buybacks, although the company's dividend payout ratio is high. This eschewing of buybacks is consistent with the increased attention of AZN's management to investment in innovation in recent years.

In five years after the merger of Astra and Zeneca in 1999, AZN was in sound financial condition, as it constrained distributions to shareholders (see Figure 11). In the two years following the MedImmune acquisition in 2007, AZN launched an 'Enhancing Productivity' restructuring programme, resulting in a 9 per cent growth in the company's net earnings. To achieve this result, AZN controlled the growth of cost items in major operational units except R&D. At the time, however, under Brennan as CEO, AZN became very shareholder-value oriented, distributing nearly £24.8 billion in cash to shareholders from 2006 to 2012. This shareholder payout amount was 2.3 times greater than that which was done by the company under McKillop from 1999 to 2005.

Although the company suspended its buyback programme in 2008–9 (as was usual among large companies during the financial crisis), AZN resumed buybacks from 2010 to 2012, spending £7.2 billion to repurchase its own shares. Towards mid-2012, amidst rising shareholder concerns about the lack of new product development, Brennan's tenure as CEO abruptly came to an end. Certain longer-term shareholders, led by Woodford, realised that without

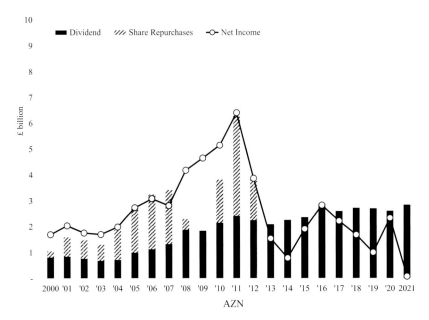

Figure 11 Value extraction: distributions to shareholders (£ billion), 2000–21, by AZN

Source: Authors' analysis and graphic based on S&P Capital IQ and company annual reports.

a renewal of sales revenues through new product launches, the distributions to shareholders that had been made over the previous years could not be sustained.

4.4 Executive Compensation

Senior executives may favour distributions to shareholders because they receive stock-based pay, usually in the form of stock options or stock awards, that incentivise them to increase stock yields. As a result, senior executive remuneration schemes, and particularly the mode of compensating the CEO, may influence the tension between innovation and financialisation.

Figure 12 shows the changing levels and components of executive pay for McKillop, Brennan, and Soriot. In 2021, the fixed portion of CEO total annual remuneration (TAR) was made up of *base salary* (£1,367,002), *other benefits* (£123,000), and *CEO post-employment (pension) benefits* (£146,000). The fixed portion declined from 79 per cent in 2004, when the PSP programme was introduced, to 29 per cent in 2011, just before Brennan retired from AZN. The fixed portion of TAR increased to 40 per cent in 2013 when Soriot became AZN's top executive before declining to 14 per cent in 2021 as Soriot's share-based compensation began to vest.

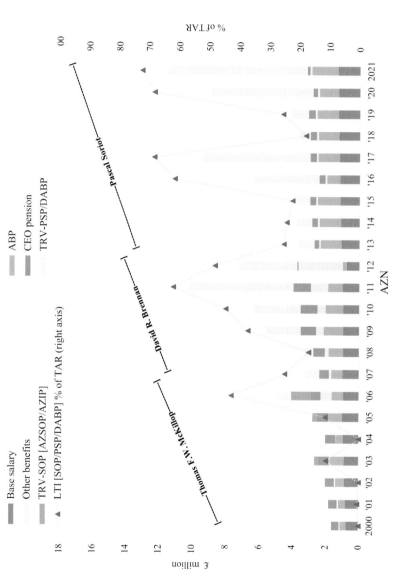

Figure 12 Changing composition of CEO pay at AZN, 2000–21

Notes: Annual Bonus Plan [ABP], AstraZeneca Investment Plan [AZIP], AstraZeneca Share Option Plan [AZSOP], Deferred Annual Bonus Plan [DABP], Long-term Incentive [LTI], Performance Share Plan [PSP], Share Option Plan [SOP], Total Annual Remuneration [TAR], and Total Realised Value [TRV].
Source: Authors' analysis and graphic based on S&P ExecuComp.

At AZN, in the early 2000s, the components of base pay, including salary, pension, and other taxable benefits, collectively accounted for nearly two-thirds of total CEO remuneration. The only variable pay component was the annual bonus plan (ABP). Independently of base and variable pay, the AZN board occasionally granted stock options to senior executives under the AstraZeneca Share Option Plan (AZSOP).

As a long-term incentive (LTI) programme, AZSOP was introduced in 2000 to replace the Zeneca 1994 Executive Share Option Scheme. AZSOP was designed for a ten-year period. To determine the number of options to grant to a senior executive under AZSOP, the board considered the overall performance of the company at the time the options were granted in terms of three broad performance measures: (a) the prospects for sales growth, (b) the launch of new products in the four years prior to the grant, and (c) savings achieved during this period through restructuring ('synergy benefits').

Although AZN used company performance criteria in deciding to *grant* stock options to senior executives, it did not impose any performance criteria for the *vesting* of these options – apparently following US practice (Hopkins and Lazonick 2016). In the United Kingdom, performance measures for the vesting of options are called 'testing' performance conditions. This issue was raised by some larger shareholders at the 2003 annual general meeting (AGM), but, with AZN's stock price in a slump, it was a moot point because previously granted options were 'under water' (i.e., the market price was less than the grant price at which the options could be exercised).

In the context of searching for a replacement for Barnevik, who retired as chairman in 2004, the board sought shareholder feedback for 'formulating proposals which focus upon performance-related pay' and that 'strengthened the links to measures which are aligned to the creation of shareholder value' (AstraZeneca 2004, p. 63). Following these discussions, in July 2004, the remuneration committee appointed Carol Arrowsmith, head of the remuneration division at Deloitte & Touche, a prominent consultancy, to advise the committee on matters concerning executive pay.

The result was an ABP awarded as part of the short-term incentive (STI) programme, accounting for no less than 14 per cent of total CEO remuneration. Subject to achieving the three performance targets, the company CEO could receive up to 180 per cent of his or her salary as an annual bonus under each plan year. Among the changes introduced to the ABP in 2004, upon meeting such goals, only two-thirds of the bonus amount is payable in cash, with the remaining one-third taking the form of the company's common shares under the deferred bonus plan (DBP). Awards deferred under DBP are subject to an additional three-year holding period, although no additional performance conditions are applied. In 2004, AZN also instituted a share ownership requirement (SOR), whereby the CEO had to accumulate and hold company shares valued at one full-year salary during and beyond employment.

In 2005, the AZN directors introduced a new set of testing performance conditions to determine when and to what extent the senior corporate leaders were authorised to exercise previously granted options. The new performance measures included an *earnings per share* (EPS) target, which rewarded senior executives for increases in EPS by 5 per cent more than the UK retail price index for each three-year performance period.

During the first implementation period from 2005 to 2008, performance share pay (PSP) was based on the relative performance of AZN's 'total shareholder return' (TSR) over the three-year period following each award in comparison with the TSR performance of twelve major pharmaceutical companies. The initial awards granted under PSP could be as much as 125 per cent of the CEO's base salary and the vesting percentage would depend on the relative TSR performance against a selected pharmaceuticals peer group (PPG) of twelve companies. The vesting metric ranges from 30 per cent of salary, if the company's TSR ranked at the median, to 100 per cent, if it ranked in the upper quartile. The remuneration committee has the discretion to award an additional 25 per cent if the company's TSR ranked significantly above the comparison group.

As a performance measure for the vesting of PSP awards, a cumulative free cash flow (FCF) target was introduced in 2008, in part to address 'shareholder concern' over the company's declining cash flow following the MedImmune acquisition. The vesting of one-half of the maximum option awards granted under PSP was subject to achieving a pre-defined FCF during the three-year performance period. These cumulative cash-flow targets have changed, depending on the company's projected performance in the product market, ranging anywhere from $8.5 to $23 billion.

At the company's AGM in 2010, following the expiration of AZSOP, AZN shareholders approved a major overhaul of the company's LTI programme. In addition to PSP, the AstraZeneca Investment Plan (AZIP), a newly adopted share-based employee incentive programme, became a major component of the company's LTI programme. AZIP was approved for an eight-year implementation period, including a four-year performance period for granting an additional four-year holding period for vesting of share awards.

During the first period, the board measures performance based on two indicators to determine the vesting percentage of maximum share awards granted at the start of the performance period. Unlike its predecessor, the extent to which the new share options granted under AZIP vest depends on the company's ability to sustain a progressive dividend payout policy. In addition to meeting the dividend per share targets determined previously, the vesting of option awards at the maximum level also depends on maintaining a dividend cover ratio (DCR), requiring the company's core EPS to be 1.5 times greater than per share dividend paid in each year during the performance period.

As AZN's structure of executive pay changed over the 2000s, the performance criteria for granting annual bonuses and stock awards became more focused on financial targets based on company stock-price movements. This pressure to adopt a more financialised remuneration policy that encourages value extraction by shareholders, however, was counterbalanced by a group of institutional shareholders who had a more patient and stable view of the need for value creation. Over the course of the 2010s, these 'value-creating' shareholders exerted influence over the design of the company's remuneration policy.

As displayed in Figure 13, relative TSR performance determines the amount of LTI for senior executives. TSR is a measure that reflects the price appreciation of company shares as well as the per-share dividends paid to the holders of the company's ordinary shares in any given year. During the first five-year implementation period following its launch in 2005, the company's relative TSR performance against PPG entirely determined the number of shares granted under PSP.

Although core EPS was introduced as a performance condition for any share option to be granted under AZSOP, the board also decided to reduce the weight of core EPS (100 per cent for CEO and 80 per cent for other senior executives). In addition, between 2005 and 2010, the board implemented a variety of qualitative and quantitative measures in the performance-evaluation process to determine the amount of ABP.

The company ceased to grant new AZIP awards in 2016, leaving PSP as the only programme that AZN implements as an LTI. Unlike its predecessor AZSOP, vesting of awards granted under AZIP was subject to achieving a dividend payout target during a four-year performance period. One-fourth of LTI awards granted under AZIP lapsed each year when AZN failed to achieve the DCR target set for that year. During the 2010s, this remuneration policy encouraged senior executives to support the company's generous dividend payout policy despite severe cash-flow problems, and as a result the LTI awards granted under AZIP rarely lapsed.

No new awards have been granted under AZIP since 2016; the company phased out AZIP, with the vesting of the last awards on 31 December 2019. The holding period for the vested awards is set to expire in 2024. Typically, within the total awards granted under LTI, AZIP awards account for 25 per cent while PSP makes up the remaining 75 per cent. Vesting of AZIP awards is subject to achieving two performance targets: AZN must pay a minimum of $2.80 dividend per share (DPS) and achieve 1.5 DCR, which requires core EPS to be 1.5 times greater than DPS.

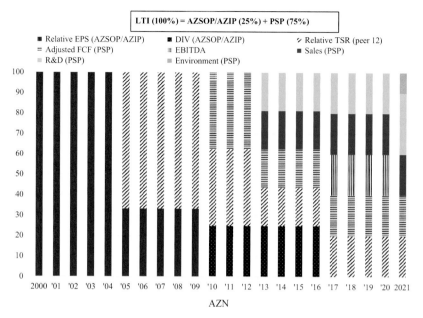

Figure 13 Weights assigned by the AZN Remuneration Committee to different financial-performance and productive-performance targets in the long-term incentive (LTI) component of remuneration for CEOs at AZN, 2000–21

Notes: AstraZeneca Investment Plan [AZIP], AstraZeneca Share Option Plan [AZSOP], Earnings Before Interest, Tax, Depreciation, and Amortisation [EBITDA], Earnings Per Share [EPS], Dividends [DIV], Free Cash Flow [FCF], Performance Share Plan [PSP], and Total Shareholder Return [TSR].
Source: Authors' analysis and graphic based on company annual reports.

In 2020, AZN adopted a number of changes to the company's CEO remuneration policy. While the CEO pension contribution decreased from 30 per cent to 20 per cent of the base salary, the maximum award for the annual bonus increased from 180 per cent to 200 per cent of base salary. Also, for the grants awarded under the ABP in 2020 and subsequent years, the board has increased the mandatory deferral from one-third to 50 per cent of the total annual bonuses received. Along with the increase of maximum award opportunity under PSP to 550 per cent of the base salary, the shareholding requirement for the CEO has been increased from 300 per cent to 550 per cent of the base salary. The most notable recent change in the remuneration policy is that the CEO and other senior executives are required to maintain 100 per cent of their shareholding during the two-year period following the termination of their employment.

Looking back two decades, by setting various TSR goals for senior executives to maximise their variable pay, the company's stock-market performance became a top managerial priority. AZN's TSR outperformed the FTSE 100 Index in 2005, but during almost the entire tenure of Brennan as CEO, the company lagged behind both the FTSE 100 index companies and its pharma peers in terms of delivering higher shareholder yields.

Rising shareholder dissent against the ever-growing remuneration of CEOs at a number of UK companies, including AZN, has had an impact on government legislation. As UK lawmakers were getting ready to pass the *Enterprise and Regulatory Reform Act of 2013,* a major provision of which would allow shareholders to cast a *binding* vote on remuneration policy every three years, growing shareholder sentiment against executive pay led to the 'shareholder spring of 2012', and the ousting of several CEOs of major publicly listed companies, both in the United States and the United Kingdom.

Disappointed with the company's innovative productivity under Schweitzer and Brennan, in 2012, as part of the UK's shareholder spring (Pratley 2012), a number of influential holders of AZN shares, led by Woodford, increased pressure on the company directors to replace the AZN chairman of the board and CEO (Evans 2014). Anticipating that his pay package would be voted down at the AGM in April 2012, Brennan pre-emptively announced his decision to retire by June 2012 (Burgess and McCrum 2012; Kollewe 2012).

Since he became CEO in October 2012, Soriot has had a clear mandate to move AZN from financialisation towards innovation. Yet, his pay package at AZN still reflects a legacy of financialisation, with its various components of stock-based pay. Given Soriot's innovation mandate, however, AZN introduced pay-performance targets related to the clinical development of innovative drugs (*Innovative Science: First approvals and NME volume over three years* in PSP and *Innovative Science: Annual pipeline progression* in ABP) and the sales growth in various therapeutic areas (*Return to Growth* in PSP and *Deliver Growth and Therapy Area Leadership* in ABP). Each pay-performance target related to innovation and sales accounted for 20 per cent and 30 per cent of PSP and ABP awards vested in Soriot's total compensation in 2021.

Unlike AZIP, LTI awards granted under PSP are nil-cost stock options which automatically vest upon achieving a combination of financial, commercial, and innovation-based performance targets during a three-year performance period. The impact of LTI awards granted under PSP on CEO TAR is evident in Figure 12. Since 2016, following the vesting of the first PSP awards granted after joining AZN, Soriot's TAR has been rising. Similar to the AZN US Executive Performance Share Plan, the global PSP is based on the relative performance of the company's TSR over the three-year period following each award against the TSR performance of PPG. As Figure 12 shows, Soriot's annual pay dropped significantly in 2018 following his failure to achieve one of the performance targets, resulting in the lapsing of awards.

The introduction over the past decade of innovation metrics as performance criteria in determining CEO pay at AZN reflects attempts to shift the strategic orientation of the company away from the financialisation of the previous decade. It must be recognised, however, that the very existence of the stock-based components of executive pay in the form of stock options and stock awards reflects the financialisation of the business enterprise. In principle, CEOs who have the ability to envision and augment an innovation strategy should not require stock-based incentives to do their jobs. Senior executives of the business corporation are employees in leadership positions who, as professionals, should be able and willing to perform at the highest possible level for a good salary and, for extraordinary outcomes, a bonus that reflects, as well, the salary/bonus structure of others in the company's hierarchical and functional division of labour.

5 GlaxoSmithKline

5.1 Strategy and Learning

In 1996, a year after acquiring Wellcome Laboratories to become the second largest pharmaceutical company in the world, Glaxo Wellcome chairman, Richard Sykes, met with the CEO of SKB, Jan Leschly, to initiate discussions about a possible merger. The $70-billion deal, considered to be the 'the mother of all mergers', sent shockwaves through the industry as it threatened to oust Merck & Co. as the global leader in pharmaceuticals (Heracleous and Murray 2001). The talks were suddenly suspended, however, with initial reports citing personality clashes between Sykes and Leschly about leadership positions, while, later, evidence emerged that pointed towards cultural differences in managerial direction as the source of termination (Randles 2002, pp. 346–9; Batiz-Lazo 2004, pp. 75–89).

In a highly perceptive essay, Tony Corley (2010, p. 235) notes 'a struggle over the direction which the pair should take, whether to pursue British- or American-type strategies'. He goes on to state: 'Sykes' basically British approach was to spend as much as possible [on R&D]', and he adds: ' . . . a policy of maximizing research activity was expected to take precedence over financial and marketing considerations' (Corley 2010). Leschly 'pursued a more money-saving policy, in the main following the American-based Pfizer's recent practices'. This approach included concentrating production in five therapeutic categories; economising on R&D expenditure by acquiring products from small biotech companies to further develop and market; establishing co-partnerships with larger competitors to gain access to therapeutic areas that it did not already dominate; and launching smaller research teams in an effort to increase flexibility, creativity, and personal initiative (Corley 2010).

The dramatic dissolution of merger talks between Sykes and Leschly in 1998 occurred against the backdrop of extensive changes in the competitive structure of the global pharmaceutical industry, with M&A activity among large, established pharmaceutical companies beginning to surge in the late 1990s. The 1999 merger of Germany-based Hoechst and France-based Rhône-Poulenc briefly positioned the merged company Aventis in the top global spot. Pfizer, however, became the world's largest pharmaceutical company following the completion of its $112 billion takeover of Warner-Lambert in 1999. Amidst consolidation in the pharmaceutical industry in 1999, Sykes and Leschly came together once again to talk about a potential merger between the two pharmaceutical companies (Corley 2010, p. 236).

After obtaining regulatory and shareholder approvals to complete the $76 billion merger deal on 27 December 2000, GSK became the world's largest pharmaceutical company. Over the last two centuries, GSK evolved through the merger of several companies which originated in the United Kingdom, New Zealand, and the United States (see Figure 14). GSK's roots in the United Kingdom can be traced back to three drug makers: Allen and Hanburys, Burroughs Wellcome & Company, and Beecham Group (see Jones 2007). SKB founded in 1989 and Glaxo Wellcome (GW) founded in 1995 merged to create GSK in 2000, with 40 per cent and 60 per cent shares, respectively, in the new company. Among companies included in Figure 3, GSK's pharmaceutical sales were only exceeded by those of Pfizer and Merck, while outperforming other major companies such as Bristol-Myers Squibb, Novartis, Eli Lilly, and Roche.

Shortly before the merger, Leschly announced his decision to retire, which paved the way for Sykes to become the non-executive chairman of the combined entity. As a result of merger negotiations, GW executives secured three of the top leadership positions – chief financial officer (CFO), chief operating officer (COO) & president pharmaceutical operations, and chief science & technology officer (CSTO) – in exchange for SKB's CEO, Jean-Pierre Garnier, becoming the top executive of the newly formed entity. It is important to note that GSK's first CSTO, Jim Niedel, was a GW executive who had been based in the United States.

Aside from the top corporate and R&D leadership, SKB also controlled two-thirds of the senior positions, including senior vice-presidents of legal affairs

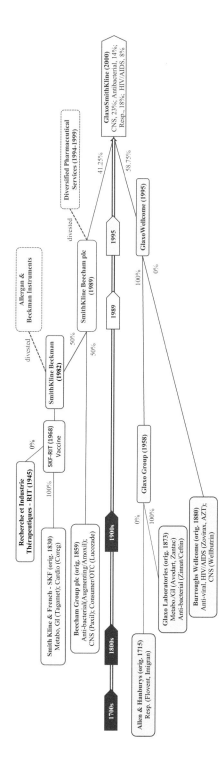

Figure 14 Pre-merger evolution of GSK

Source: Authors' own illustration based on information compiled from various sources.

and human resources, in addition to three of the five critical leadership positions in strategic business units, including president of pharmaceuticals international, US pharmaceuticals, and consumer healthcare. More importantly, SKB's head of R&D, Tachi Yamada, became the company's top scientist, overseeing GSK's global R&D operations following the merger. With Sykes as non-executive chairman of the combined entity, SKB secured strategic control of GSK, even though GW shareholders controlled 17.5 per cent more equity in GSK than SKB's.

The SKB–GW combination took the form of a nil-premium merger of equals through which the ownership of both parties was transferred into a holding company, avoiding stamp duty of over £200 million. GSK stock was listed on both the UK and US markets. With UK-based holders of Glaxo, Burroughs Wellcome, and Beecham Group maintaining their ownership stakes, it was anticipated that 85 per cent of the new GSK shares would be issued to UK-based shareholders. GSK was established as a UK-based company, thus avoiding legal issues concerning securities regulations in the United Kingdom and the United States. US-based shareholders held less than 10 per cent of GSK's outstanding shares (Birkett 2001).

GSK's global headquarters were located in London, but SKB's former headquarters in Philadelphia became GSK's administrative base because the new CEO, Garnier, wanted to remain in the United States. It was only in 2008 when Andrew Witty replaced Garnier as the first British CEO of the Anglo-American company that GSK's administrative offices were relocated to the United Kingdom.

Over the two decades since the merger, GSK has had three CEOs: Jean-Pierre Garnier, 2000–8; Andrew Witty, 2008–17; and Emma Walmsley, 2017–present. Although Garnier was from France, he had spent the 1990s as an executive in the United States, having joined SKB in 1990. He became the chief operating officer in 1995 and, just before the merger, SKB's CEO. As GSK CEO, Garnier demanded a US-style stock-option package as a condition for staying with the company. While Garnier allocated resources to innovation by investing in the internal development of high-risk specialty drugs, he also sought to boost GSK's stock price by doing large-scale buybacks in addition to dividend payments. Froud et al. (2006) examine various internal (organisational) and external (institutional) factors that resulted in GSK's disengagement with organisational learning as the company began to outsource early-discovery research and build a pipeline through partnership deals with other companies in the early 2000s. Despite high levels of R&D spending, by the second half of the decade, GSK's pipeline was not generating any blockbusters. In 2008, Garnier's pay exploded as he exercised his stock options. But GSK's stock price languished as did its innovative performance, and in 2008 the company's board ousted their first CEO.

With his departure, the GSK board appointed Witty, a long-term employee of GW, as CEO. Witty, who had stayed on at GSK as the head of marketing, had been promoted to president of GSK Europe in 2003. As GSK CEO, he was averse to continuing to invest in the company's existing pipeline of high-risk specialty drugs. Besides the uncertainty of the strategy, Witty thought that the major pharmaceutical markets, including the United States, would move to tighter regulation of prescription drug prices. He favoured investments in 'high-volume, low-price pharmaceuticals', and, towards this end, in 2015, he swapped GSK's cancer business for Novartis' vaccine unit (Ward 2015). Witty also formed a joint venture with Novartis in consumer-health products.

Witty's high-volume, low-price strategy resulted in a dramatic drop in GSK's profits and free-fall in share prices in 2016. As Figure 15 shows, while GSK's product sales increased during the period 2000–21, net income was generally flat, and, although it rose after 2016 after plunging to its lowest point in the two decades, net income was still low in 2021 both in absolute terms and relative to sales.

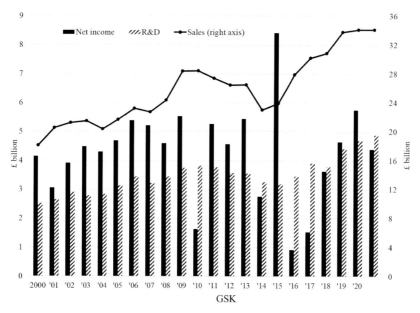

Figure 15 Product sales, net income, R&D spending at GSK (£ billion), 2000–21
Source: Authors' analysis and graphic based on S&P Capital IQ and company annual reports.

Given GSK's lacklustre performance, certain institutional shareholders demanded the spin-off of the consumer healthcare business (CHB), which Witty opposed. In February 2016, Neil Woodford, a longstanding GSK shareholder who had 7 per cent of his investment fund in GSK shares, voiced the discontent with GSK's current leadership: 'What did Einstein say? That doing the same thing over and over again and expecting a different result is the definition of madness? Well that is what Witty and the board have done for the past eight years.' (Wild 2016). In March 2016 Witty announced he would retire as CEO in the following year.

As his replacement the board appointed Emma Walmsley. She had been an executive at L'Oréal, the French personal care company, for seventeen years before she joined GSK in 2010. Walmsley had been handpicked by Witty to oversee the expansion of GSK's CHB, which was an integral part of his grand strategy to grow GSK (Fry and Zillman 2018). Given pressure in the United Kingdom for gender diversity in top corporate positions, Walmsley was a prime candidate for CEO at GSK. Indeed, shortly after his appointment as non-executive chairman of GSK in May 2015, Sir Philip Hampton, along with Dame Helen Alexander, had been commissioned by the UK government for a five-year period to conduct annual independent reviews of gender diversity in the UK-listed companies' boards of directors and senior executive teams. What became known as the Hampton-Alexander review of FTSE Women Leaders, published from 2016 through 2021, provided the framework for a voluntary code of conduct for UK-listed companies to improve gender balance in FTSE leadership. With Hampton as GSK chairman, Walmsley became the first female CEO to run any Big Pharma company.

Upon taking the helm, Walmsley vowed to 'put more discipline in place' to stop 'drifting off in hobby land', announcing the closure of thirty preclinical drug development programmes, allocation of 80 per cent of the R&D budget to be spent on no more than four strategic disease areas, and replacing 50 per cent of GSK's top management team (Neville 2017; Weintraub 2018). Figure 16 indicates that Wamsley's restructuring strategy has entailed higher value-added R&D, with R&D spending per R&D employee increasing from £300,000 in 2016 to just over £400,000 in 2021. Between 2016 and 2021, employment in manufacturing declined dramatically from 38,400 to 32,100.

While the company's clinical pipeline and sales of pharmaceutical products declined from 2010, the number of products that GSK launched increased steadily. The implications of such a disengagement are illustrated in Figure 17, showing a significant increase in GSK's early-clinical pipeline (phases 1 & 2), while the number of projects in the preclinical stage appears to be stagnating. Our analysis of GSK's changing drug-development activities

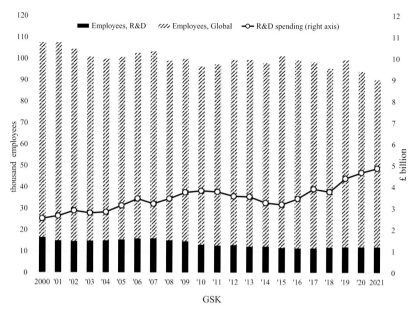

Figure 16 R&D spending (in £ billion), global employees and R&D employees at GSK, 2000–21

Source: Authors' analysis and graphics based on company annual reports.

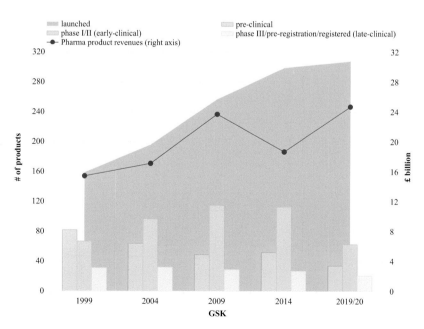

Figure 17 GSK's pharmaceutical products sales (£ billion), number of products launched and under development (pre-, early-, and late-clinical stages), FY1999–3Q2020

Source: Authors' analysis and graphic based on Pharmaprojects.

indicates a strategy to downsize in-house discovery research in favour of research geared more towards the clinical development and commercialisation of products acquired from external partners.

GSK's pace of transition from innovation to financialisation increased significantly through the mid-2010s, underpinning the company's ongoing productivity crisis. As we have seen, however, with Walmsley as CEO, an attempt at reversal has been in progress since 2017.

5.2 Innovation through In-House Development and Acquisition

At GSK, intangible assets accounted for 51 per cent of the company's total assets at the end of 2021. Figure 18 shows GSK's cumulative growth of tangible assets, goodwill, and other intangible assets in relation to total net debt since 2000. The cumulative growth of GSK's goodwill was significantly higher than the company's other intangible assets from 2007.

With the exception of the significant drop in 2014, a reflection of the company's divestment of oncology products, the overall growth in the value of GSK's goodwill and other intangible assets is striking, with a major increase between 2018 and 2019 under Walmsley due to various acquisitions, including

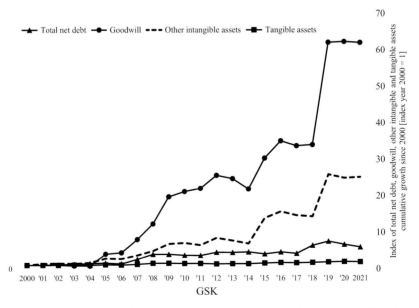

Figure 18 Intangible and tangible assets in relation to total net debt (£ billion) at GSK, 2000–21

Source: Authors' analysis and graphic based on S&P Capital IQ and company annual reports.

Tesaro (see Table 5). While the value of other intangibles increased by 9.4 times from 2004 to 2016, the value of goodwill increased by forty-three times during the same period – a reflection of the company's heightened interest in acquisitions, and the high prices paid for them, while Garnier and Witty were CEOs. In retrospect, these intangible assets were overvalued because they did not translate commensurably into higher revenues and profits.

GSK embarked on an acquisition spree in part to boost the number of new products in its portfolio, which included several products whose patents were facing expiry. Ten drugs identified in the company's 2008 *Annual Report*, which accounted for nearly 20 per cent of GSK's total product revenues and 40 per cent of pharma revenues, had patent protection in major world markets that was set to expire between 2006 and 2009. The sales of GSK's blockbuster type-2 diabetes drug, Avandia, began to plummet in 2007 following a warning letter issued by the FDA, indicating an increase in cardiovascular problems associated with its use among diabetes patients.

Figure 18 shows a sharp growth in GSK's intangible assets, the result of acquisitions, in the final years of Garnier's tenure. In anticipation of a significant decline in product sales following patent expirations, acquisitions under Garnier mainly focused on expanding the company's pipeline in high-growth product markets such as immuno-inflammation therapies as well as mature drugs such as cardiovascular and dermatology products. In 2006, when some shareholders began to show scepticism over the company's innovative productivity, GSK increased its efforts to pursue collaborative research and licensing deals valued at up to £3 billion, including upfront cash as well as milestone payments contingent upon drug candidates subject to the partnership deals. In 2006, GSK also spent £280 million in cash to expand the company's consumer health product portfolio, with its acquisitions including CNR, Inc., the US-based developer of popular healthcare products such as *Breathe Right* nasal strips and *FiberChoice* dietary fibre supplements.

Following the leadership transition from Garnier to Witty in 2009, GSK stepped up its efforts to further expand its dermatology business with the acquisition of US-based Stiefel Laboratories, paying £2.5 billion in cash for the world's largest dermatological pharmaceutical company (see Table 5). This acquisition not only resulted in the further growth of the company's intangible assets but also enhanced GSK's commercial infrastructure in major emerging drug markets.

In the following years, under Witty, GSK's market growth strategy swiftly shifted towards acquisitions with revenue-generating drugs that would help the company to replace products for which patent expiry loomed ahead. As Figure 18 shows, GSK's intangible assets took a sharp downturn in 2014 following the decision to divest certain brands in the consumer health division (also see Table 5).

Table 5 Selected acquisition, licensing, and divestments deals at GSK, 2000–21

		GSK Selected M&A (deals for value disclosed)			
			Total Value (£ million)		
CEO	**Year**	**Acquisition target/acquirer**	**Acquired**	**Divested**	**Capabilities acquired/divested**
Jean-Pierre Garnier	**2001**	Quest Diagnostics [shares already own]		188	Diagnostics
		Block Drug Company, Inc.	1,039		Dental consumer health and OTC products
	2002	Theravance (fka Advanced Medicine) minority	n.d.		Respiratory
	2004	Sanofi-Synthelabo's Arixtra and Fraxiparine	302		Drug therapies for cardiovascular disease
	2005	Corixa	185		Immuno-inflammatory and vaccine products
		ID Biomedical	849		vaccines
	2006	CNS, Inc.	305		Consumer health and OTC products
	2007	Domantis	230		Monoclonal antibodies
		Reliant	1,337		Cardiovascular
	2008	Sirtris	365		Diabetes and anti-ageing therapies
Andew Witty	**2009**	Quest Diagnostics [shares already own]		115	Diagnostics
		Wellbutrin XL and other assets by Aspen		579	Central nervous system
		UCB [limited commercial rights]	482		Various pharmaceutical and OTC products

Year	Acquisition / Disposal			Description
	TIKA [AZN's OTC products unit]	146		OTC products
	Stiefel Laboratories	2,477		Dermatology
2010	Amplimmune [product asset only]	320		Oncology
	Innoviva (fka Theravance) [increased equity]	83		Respiratory
	Laboratorios Phoenix	173		Sales and marketing in Latin America
2011	Cellzome [remaining 80% equity]	61		Technology platform for drug R&D
	MaxiNutrition Limited	166		Consumer health and OTC products
2012	Pharmaceutical and OTC assets by Aspen		328	Twenty-five legacy pharma and non-core OTC products
	OTC products by Prestige Brands		421	Seventeen OTC products
	Welicham Biotech	135		specialised immuno-inflammatory
	Basilea Pharmaceuticals	196		Anti-cancer and dermatology products
	Human Genome Sciences	2,355		Oncology and other drug therapies
2013	Anti-coagulant products business by Aspen		274	Anti-coagulant products business
	Lucozade and Ribena brands by Suntory		1,057	Consumer products
	Okairos	214		Vaccine products
	GSK Pharma India [partial equity]	577		Ownership increased in the joint venture
2014	RVT-101 by Axovant		111	Alzheimer's drug candidate
	Production site in France by Aspen		600	Sterile production site
	GSK Pharma India [partial equity]	635		Ownership increased in the joint venture
2015	OTC brands by Perrigo		148	Legacy OTC brands

Table 5 (cont.)

GSK Selected M&A (deals for value disclosed)

CEO	Year	Acquisition target/acquirer	Total Value (£ million)		Capabilities acquired/divested
			Acquired	Divested	
		GSK's equity stake in Aspen by Aspen		571	South African pharmaceutical company
		GSK's oncology unit by Novartis		9,510	Oncology assets including AKT inhibitor
		GlycoVaxyn AG	125		rDNA vaccine
		Novartis AG [global vaccines business]	4,190		Various vaccine products excluding influenza
	2016	BristolMyersSquibb [HIV R&D assets]	1,948		Discovery, preclinical, and late-stage candidates
		Anaesthetics products portfolio by Aspen		280	Anaesthetics
Emma Walmsley	2018	Consumer health JV [Novartis AG's 36.5 per cent]	9,153		Consumer Healthcare Business
		23andMe [partial equity]	229		Drug discovery partnership
		Horlicks and other brands by Unilever		3,100	Consumer and other nutritional products
		Tesaro	4,000		Oncology R&D platform and assets
	2019	Haleon JV with Pfizer, spinoff [68 per cent]		n.a.	Consumer health and OTC products
		Sitari Pharmaceuticals from Avalon Ventures	n.d.		Autoimmune (Celiac) disease

Year	Company			Focus
2020	Lyell Immunopharma [partial equity]	203		Cancer cell therapies
	Vir Biotechnology [partial equity]	204		Anti-viral antibodies for COVID-19
	CureVac [partial equity]	234		mRNA-based vaccines and mAbs
	Surface Oncology [partial equity]	63		Immuno-oncology
	Adrestia Therapeutics [partial equity]			DNA repair (Disease Rebalancing Platform)
2021	Innoviva equity stake by Innoviva		277	Respiratory
	iTeos Therapeutics	443		Immuno-oncology
	Alector	508		Immuno-neurology for neurodegenerative disorders
	Sierra Oncology	1,449		Immuno-oncology
2001–21	Other divestitures		6,192	
Total from selected acquisitions/divestitures 2000–21		**35,381**	**23,751**	

In the two markets, anti-infectives and respiratory drugs, in which GSK had been a major competitor in the past, the company entered into a licensing agreement with Galapagos in 2010. In the same year, GSK acquired one-quarter of Theravance's equity shares, in part to secure the future commercial rights to Relvar/Breo Ellipta and Anoro Ellipta, asthma drugs that the two companies had co-developed through an R&D partnership established in 2002, with the expectation of completing late-stage clinical studies in 2012. Under Witty, GSK's product-market strategy took another swift turn in 2015 following the decision to swap several assets in the company's oncology drugs portfolio for the assets in Novartis' consumer health division.

In 2008, when Witty had taken over as CEO, GSK held 22 per cent of the market for global HIV medicines, estimated at £6.4 billion. Of the six HIV products that GSK marketed in 2008, four drugs, accounting for 60 per cent of GSK's HIV product revenues, would lose patent protection in major drug markets by 2016. The market leader was Gilead Sciences, whose four HIV drugs accounted for 43 per cent of the HIV drug market in 2008. The patents on the four Gilead drugs were set to expire in the US or European drug markets on dates ranging from 2017 to 2021. In response to the competitive pressure from Gilead Sciences, in 2009 GSK and Pfizer agreed to consolidate their HIV assets into a UK-based joint-venture, ViiV. Shionogi, a Japanese pharmaceutical company, later became a partner in ViiV. The joint venture competed with Gilead by offering cocktail therapies that combine existing drugs of the three companies, despite the fact that most of the individual active ingredients of the therapy combinations are no longer under patent protection (Gupta et al. 2010). In vaccines, GSK acquired two Switzerland-based companies: Okairos in 2013 for its clinical pipeline of vaccines for infectious diseases such as hepatitis C and certain cancer types, and GlycoVaxyn in 2015 for its highly sophisticated vaccine-development capabilities.

GSK was also positioned to enter the field of genomics. Prior to its merger with GW in 2000, SKB had begun exploring opportunities for validating targets as researchers gained more insights into the biological knowledge of various diseases made available by advances in the field of genomics. In 1993, SKB entered a new partnership with Human Genome Sciences (HGS), founded in Rockville, Maryland, the previous year, for the co-development of HGS's novel drug therapies for auto-immune, cardiovascular, and metabolic diseases (McNamee and Ledley 2013). Through the continuation of this collaboration with HGS, GSK gained access to capabilities in this new field. In 2011, the R&D partnership between GSK and HGS resulted in the approval of Benlysta, the first and only approved treatment for lupus. GSK completed the £2.4 billion acquisition of HGS in 2012. Of the five mid- or late-stage clinical candidates acquired from HGS, Tanzeum, for the treatment of diabetes, was the only drug to win regulatory approval. Approved by the FDA in 2014, Tanzeum was withdrawn in 2017, however, following its disappointing sales performance due to safety concerns.[5]

Ultimately, therefore, GSK failed to take advantage of the opportunity to engage in organisational learning in the field of genomics. Noting dissatisfaction with this failure, several institutional shareholders emerged around 2015 as proponents of a major restructuring plan to transform GSK from a large health-care conglomerate into four standalone businesses specialised in distinct segments of the global healthcare market: HIV-AIDS, consumer health products, vaccines, and pharmaceuticals (Romeo 2015). The institutional shareholders became particularly disgruntled when, in 2015, CEO Witty swapped GSK's oncology unit for Novartis' vaccine division, while agreeing with Novartis to merge the consumer healthcare businesses of the two companies into a non-traded joint venture, with 63.5 per cent of its votes controlled by GSK. As a large GSK shareholder, Woodford criticised Witty for 'a misalignment ... between Glaxo and its shareholders', reflecting in his view a more general disdain among shareholders for GSK's diminishing innovative capabilities (Woodford 2017).

After Walmsley replaced Witty, she initially refused to break up the company (Hirschler 2017). Dissatisfied with this position, on 12 May 2017, Woodford issued a public statement with the title 'GLAXIT', in which he stated he would sell the GSK stake that he had held for 17 years (Woodford 2017). Led by Woodford, the advocates for demerger had argued that corporate leadership at GSK had lost its strategic focus as a pharmaceutical company and that both the consumer healthcare division and the pharmaceutical division would gain by becoming separate units of strategic control. They argued that GSK had become increasingly dependent on its HIV/AIDS franchise to sustain its profit margin. Furthermore, revenue growth in the consumer healthcare and vaccines divisions had helped top management offset the decline in pharmaceutical-division revenues as several pharma products in the company's fast-ageing portfolio began to lose market share following the launch of innovative new therapies by competitors.

The new product strategy adopted while Witty was at the helm may have helped the company to stabilise revenue growth overall, by stopping the haemorrhaging of sales in the pharma division. That strategy, however, appears to have

---

[5] In December 2012, GSK was granted regulatory approval of Abthrax (raxibacumab), which was the first and only biologics for the treatment of anthrax at the time of its approval. Raxibacumab was a clinical asset which GSK had acquired from HGS only a few months before the drug won regulatory approval. When GSK decided to withdraw Tanzeum from the market in July 2017, the company also sold the global rights of raxibacumab.

also eliminated any sense of urgency for the pharma division to reinvigorate its clinical pipeline by engaging in new learning that could place the company on a more sustainable growth path as a pharmaceutical company. While Witty persisted in dismissing the idea of splitting up GSK, several global drug companies were in the process of, or had already completed, major shifts in product strategies that focused on innovative drug therapies. For instance, since 2009, when Roche fully acquired Genentech, a company in which it had held a majority stake since 1990, Roche's product strategy has focused on developing highly innovative specialised biopharma therapies and companion diagnostics. In 2013, Abbott Laboratories spun-out its pharma division to form a standalone company, AbbVie, which focuses solely on developing novel biopharmaceutical therapies. As we discussed in the previous section of this Element, with Soriot as CEO since 2012, AZN has transformed itself into an innovative biopharma company, focusing mainly on the development of high-value-added specialty pharmaceuticals such as immuno-oncology products.

During the final year of his tenure as CEO, Witty repeatedly denied the claims that his decision to retire sooner than anticipated was because the board wanted a new CEO who would be favourable to the idea of pursuing the demergers of GSK's pharmaceutical and consumer healthcare businesses (Hirschler 2016). Early in her tenure as CEO, Walmsley appeared to be aligned with Witty on this issue. In fact, she revealed that when she was head of CHB GSK was considering the option of acquiring some of Pfizer's non-pharma assets to create the world's largest consumer healthcare business under GSK (Bradshaw 2018). Discussions of this acquisition plan were dropped, however, when several institutional shareholders raised concerns over the impact of a $25-billion acquisition on the company's near-term cash flows, with the possibility that GSK would be financially constrained in achieving dividend payout targets (Hirschler 2017).

Unlike Witty, however, Walmsley championed a major change in innovation strategy in the pharma division by means of the transformation of R&D leadership and re-organisation of global R&D operations. Walmsley initiated the organisational transformation process with the appointment of Hal Barron as GSK's top scientist. A world-renowned cancer researcher, Barron had previously led the R&D organisations of Genentech/Roche and Calico, Google's healthcare technology venture. As a condition of his employment, Barron insisted on keeping California as his base in order to remain embedded within one of the world's most productive biomedical innovation ecosystems.

Barron recognised the importance of increasing genetically validated targets to improve the clinical success rate. To implement this strategy, he initiated a culture shift in R&D to focus on projects with significantly greater scientific understanding rather than the previous volume-based approach to assess the efficiency of R&D. Based on this orientation, GSK has entered into a new strategic partnership with 23andMe, a California-based developer of genetic test-kits, allowing GSK to explore the vast database of genetic information collected by 23andMe from, in 2021, 12 million individuals (Mullard 2019; 23andMe 2021).

With Walmsley's support, Barron also sought to turn GSK into a major player in the market for immuno-oncology products. In 2019, GSK became engaged in the highly innovative Massachusetts biopharma sector through its £4.0 billion acquisition of Tesaro, a company in the Boston area with several late-stage oncology assets.

With this renewed focus on pharma innovation, Walmsley was now ready to spin off consumer healthcare as a separate company. In December 2018, GSK agreed to a major joint-venture deal with Pfizer to consolidate their consumer product businesses into what would become the world's largest consumer healthcare company. Named Haleon plc, the standalone company was de-merged on 18 July 2022. Against the objection of Elliott Management, Walmsley succeeded in remaining CEO of GSK, with the pharma company's financial position strengthened by offloading over ten billion pounds.

Overseeing the launch of Haleon as GSK chairman is Jonathan Symonds, who in September 2019 replaced Hampton. Symonds was a financial executive at Zeneca when he became centrally involved in the merger with Astra in 2000. He was appointed the AZN CFO in 2001 and was seen as a top candidate to become the company's CEO. In 2007, however, AZN's directors decided to replace retiring CEO McKillop with Brennan (Hirschler 2007). As a result, Symonds left AZN for Goldman Sachs as a transition (as it turned out) to becoming CFO of Novartis in 2009. In 2013, he became senior independent director of HSBC Holdings plc, rising to deputy chair in August 2018. He was recruited to become GSK's board chairman just over a year later. Iain Mackay, GSK's new CFO from April 2019, also came from HSBC.

What lies at the core of this turnaround strategy appears to be a major shift away from focusing on the commercialisation of significantly lower value-added products such as consumer health towards developing high value-added products, focusing on relatively fewer therapeutic areas, including immuno-oncology. Given the breadth and depth of learning required for such drug therapies, the extent to which GSK's top leadership maintains its commitment to support the required collective and cumulative learning efforts will determine the success of the company's new innovation strategy.

5.3 Distributions to Shareholders

Through its two decades of existence, GSK has had a strong focus on extracting value for shareholders. As Figure 19 shows, following the merger in 2000, GSK's dividend payments continued growing steadily reaching a peak in 2016, in the same year when the company's net income reached a twenty-year low. In 2017 to 2021, GSK reduced its dividends back to the level where they had been in 2012 to 2015. In addition, GSK did stock buybacks from 2000 to 2014, with buybacks surpassing dividends in 2007 and 2008 before cutting them out completely during the financial crisis of 2009 and 2010. GSK resumed buybacks from 2011, but in 2014 announced that it would be doing much less buybacks in favour of dividends in the future. After 2017, when GSK had to reduce its dividends from their peak in 2016, the company ceased doing buybacks.

In July 2007, shortly after the publication of a new study that revealed higher risk associated with the use of Avandia – the major type-2 diabetes drug launched in 2003 that had reached blockbuster status of £1.1 billion in revenues in 2004 – GSK's board approved a £12-billion share-repurchase programme, double the size of the programme authorised in 2006, to be completed over the

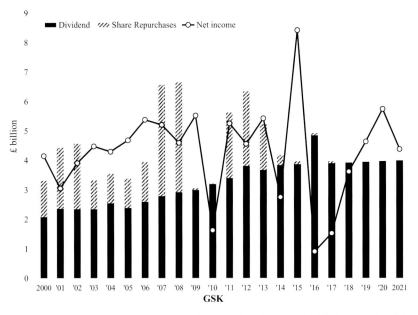

Figure 19 Value extraction: distributions to shareholders (£ billion), 2000–21, by GSK

Source: Authors' analysis and graphic based on S&P Capital IQ and company annual reports.

next two years. With the company's stock price declining sharply following the release of an FDA warning letter restricting the use of Avandia, GSK repurchased £7.5 billion in 2007 and 2008 in an attempt to offset the stock-price decline.

These large-scale repurchases contributed to the inflation of Garnier's pay as he was retiring as CEO on May 2008. The high levels of payouts as dividends and buybacks under Garnier contributed to the quadrupling in GSK's total net debt, from £4.0 billion in 2000 to £16.2 billion by the end of 2008. Nearly 72 per cent of the new debt was issued in 2007 and 2008 to finance the stock buybacks (see Figures 18 and 19).

In 2010, amid escalating Avandia safety concerns following the additional clinical evidence reported by independent studies, the FDA finally decided to restrict the use of this drug while the marketing of Avandia had been halted by the European drug regulatory agency, citing the mounting evidence of cardiovascular risk. During the marketing of Avandia, from the first approval in 1999 to its withdrawal globally in 2012, cumulative sales of Avandia products were over £10 billion. With the US and European regulators suspending the use of Avandia in 2009 and 2010, GSK took a provision of £4.8 billion for settlement of potential civil and criminal charges. In 2010, GSK's net income went down to a record low of £1.6 billion. Under these circumstances, GSK decided that, whatever was happening to its stock prices, it could not afford to do buybacks.

Following the divestment of oncology as well as various pharmaceutical and consumer health assets from 2014, GSK's total debt decreased from £18.8 billion in 2014 to £17.1 billion in 2017. In anticipation of the prospective joint-venture arrangement with Pfizer to consolidate its consumer health assets in a jointly owned subsidiary, GSK issued £9.9 billion in new debt in 2018 to acquire Novartis' 36.5 per cent equity stake in GSK's consumer health division.

5.4 Executive Compensation

In 2021, the fixed portion of the CEO's total annual remuneration (TAR) was made up of base salary (£1,223,160), other benefits (£134,000), and CEO post-employment (pension) benefits (£245,000). As Figure 20 shows, this fixed proportion declined from 60 per cent in 2002, when the Performance Share Plan (PSP) programme was introduced, to 26 per cent in 2016 when Witty retired from GSK. The fixed proportion of the CEO TAR increased to 44.8 per cent in 2021 as Walmsley's share-based compensation granted under Share Option Plan (SOP), Deferred Annual Bonus Plan (DABP), and PSP was still subject to performance and holding conditions before realising any gains.

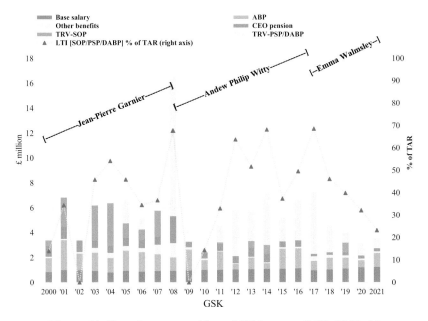

Figure 20 Changing composition of CEO pay at GSK, 2000–21

Notes: Annual Bonus Plan [ABP], Deferred Annual Bonus Plan [DABP], Long-term Incentive [LTI], Performance Share Plan [PSP], Share Option Plan [SOP], Total Annual Remuneration [TAR], Total Realised Value [TRV].
Source: Authors' analysis and graphic based on S&P ExecuComp.

Since GSK ceased granting new stock options to executive directors under SOP in 2009, the total value realised from exercising options (TRV-SOP) has been limited. Note also that the remuneration shown for 2008 combines that received by Garnier and Witty, with Garnier capturing all the realised gains from stock awards (TRV-PSP/DABP) at the end of his tenure. Similarly, the total remuneration for 2017 combines pay received by Witty and Walmsley, with Witty reaping all the gains from stock awards.

Since the merger in 1999, with the implementation of new corporate governance practices, CEO pay at GSK has taken on a highly complex structure as the board has introduced a number of new pay components, many features of which reflect changing views of the remuneration package needed to attract, retain, motivate, and reward the CEO. In the immediate aftermath of the merger, CEO pay consisted of a minimum base salary (BASE) that, at the discretion of the board, could be augmented by a bonus that was justified by a vague combination of criteria, including revenue growth and 'total shareholder return' (TSR). The implementation of the Combined Code in the early 2000s included stock-based 'performance' incentives for CEOs.

To bring the company's governance practices in alignment with the Combined Code, in 2002, GSK's directors divided the purview of the Remuneration and Nomination committee into two independent bodies. The newly created Remuneration Committee hired the consultancy Deloitte & Touche to evaluate the company's executive-pay policy that would be both in compliance with the Combined Code and sufficiently competitive to attract global talent.

Among the consultancy's notable policy recommendations was the change of the comparator benchmark group when determining the amounts and components of the CEO's annual pay. Deloitte & Touche argued that CEO pay at GSK was not competitively packaged to attract global talent, especially from the US-based global pharmaceutical companies that offered more generous pay packages, heavily weighted with stock-based pay. In benchmarking CEO pay at GSK, the remuneration strategies of a pharmaceutical peer group (PPG) of thirteen global companies, nine of them US-based, replaced the practice, that had been adopted in 2000, of using a group of leading FTSE-100 companies. The former benchmark had been adopted because, according to the *2002 Annual Report*, 'a number of shareholders with a UK equity mandate requested a performance measure tied to a UK equity index' (GSK 2002, p. 42).

In 2002, GSK directors introduced PSP that included TSR as the performance measure, in part to align the company's remuneration policy with PPG. The *Companies Act 2006* introduced several important corporate governance rules to regulate the duties and remuneration of corporate directors and to establish standards for the ways in which UK-listed companies were required to comply when reporting the activities of corporate directors. The interaction of the 2006 Act and the Combined Code resulted in major revisions to the company's remuneration policy in the context of a transition in GSK's top leadership in 2008.

As mandated by these new regulatory requirements, GSK's directors proposed revisions in the company's remuneration policy during the 2009 AGM. They adopted a comparison group of sixteen major UK-listed companies against which the total CEO and CFO compensation at GSK was benchmarked. As the remuneration benchmark for the chief scientific officer (CSO), however, PPG remained in effect as the remuneration benchmark. Additional revisions to the company's remuneration policy in 2009 responded to growing shareholder concerns of the ineffectiveness of the current stock-option plan to enhance executive performance.

The new remuneration policy proposed in 2009 included provisions such as a 'clawback' mechanism to ensure that poor corporate performance was not rewarded. Authorised for a ten-year implementation period following the merger in 2000, the company's expiring SOP was reauthorised in 2009 for another ten-year period for GSK employees and senior leadership. The changes introduced in the 2009 remuneration policy, however, excluded the CEO and CFO from participating in the SOP.

Since the changes introduced in 2009, LTI in CEO pay has been mainly implemented through the PSP under which the CEO can receive stock-based awards up to six times their base salary. Under the 2011 remuneration policy, the company directors introduced more comprehensive revisions, which entailed more explicit linkages between LTI performance measures and the company's key strategic objectives such as growing a diversified business, delivering more products of value, simplifying the operating models, and delivering value to shareholders (see Figure 21).

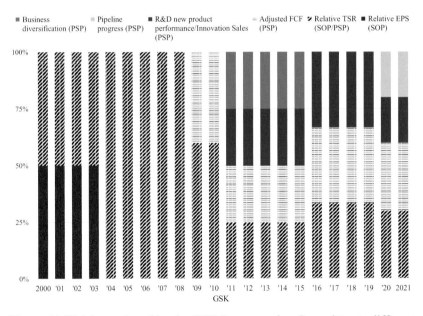

Figure 21 Weights assigned by the GSK Remuneration Committee to different financial-performance and productive-performance targets in the long-term incentive (LTI) component of remuneration for CEOs at GSK, 2000–21

Note: Earnings Per Share [EPS], Free Cash Flow [FCF], Performance Share Plan [PSP], and Total Shareholder Return [TSR].
Source: Authors' analysis and graphic based on company annual reports.

The vesting level of PSP awards that the CEO received under each plan year between 2011 and 2015 was determined by the extent to which GSK achieved a number of stretching targets in four distinct LTI performance measures: business diversification, R&D new product performance, adjusted FCF, and relative TSR, with each factor weighted in equal proportion.

Performance measures are calculated differently for each stretching target. The business diversification performance measure is an aggregate three-year revenue target to be achieved in four strategic markets: vaccines, consumer healthcare, dermatology, as well as emerging markets and Japan. The R&D new product performance measure is an aggregate three-year revenue target to be achieved in products launched any time during a five-year period, up to two years prior to the grant date and during the three-year performance period. The adjusted FCF measure is the aggregate three-year cash flow target to be achieved each year during the performance period. Relative TSR ties the vesting of up to one-quarter of LTIs to the ranking of the company's TSR performance among the top ten global pharmaceutical companies included in the PPG for benchmarking. While the vesting of awards at the maximum requires GSK's TSR performance to rank within the top three of the peer-group companies, no awards vest if the relative TSR ranked below the group median.

GSK's directors introduced several changes to the company's remuneration policy for 2013 that sought shareholder approval at the 2013 AGM. Those changes included the discontinuance of business diversification as an LTI performance measure, bringing the weight of non-financial targets within the total LTI performance measures down from one-half to one-third starting with the awards granted in 2016 (see Figure 21). Since the early 2000s, prominent UK institutional shareholders had demanded that more comprehensive and competitive performance hurdles be exceeded for the vesting of LTIs granted to UK executives to occur. These hurdles include a longer vesting or holding period before the exercise of any LTI award. The changes introduced in the 2013 remuneration policy included an additional two-year holding period after the vesting of PSP awards, following a three-year performance period.

Against a backdrop of policy debate urging major UK-listed companies to engage in long-term value creation, GSK's directors introduced significant changes to various bonus plans in the remuneration policy for 2017. The remuneration package for the new executive team under Walmsley no longer offered one-for-one matching for deferred annual bonuses, as the mandatory deferral increased from 25 per cent to 50 per cent. For the purpose of increasing accountability of senior leadership, the SOR increased from 400 per cent to 650 per cent of salary.

In 2017, the performance targets for the annual bonus were simplified: the core Group operating profit target was removed to link 70 per cent of bonus to a predefined core Group PBIT target for the award year. The vesting of the remaining 30 per cent of the annual bonus is subject to achieving pre-agreed individual objectives based on financial, sales, and R&D-related targets, paying particular attention to restructuring of R&D operations and reviving the company's clinical pipeline.

In 2019, GSK changed the benchmark groups for CEO pay and relative TSR performance as major shareholders argued that the UK cross-industry and global PPGs used for benchmarks were too narrow. The board approved a broader European cross-industry comparator group as the benchmark for the company's relative TSR performance as well as the CEO pay.

Unlike the top executives of US-based pharma companies who can typically realise gains on their stock options as soon as they are exercised and on their stock awards as soon as they vest, it may take GSK executives many years to build a shareholding that complies with SOR before they can sell some shares and realise gains. Under the new SOR rules, after termination of employment, senior GSK executives are required to maintain 100 per cent of their shareholding for the first twelve-month period and 50 per cent for the second twelve-month period. Unlike US stock-based executive pay, which enables the timing of the sale of acquired shares to realise gains from the use of stock buybacks to manipulate stock prices (Hopkins and Lazonick 2016), UK stock-based executive remuneration schemes such as that at GSK just described give senior executives a far greater interest in dividends as opposed to buybacks.

At GSK, from 2011 to 2021 at least 50 per cent of the LTI performance targets in CEO remuneration were finance-oriented rather than product-oriented, with the proportion rising as high as two-thirds from 2016 to 2019. In the company's remuneration policy for 2021, the weights of finance-oriented performance targets, relative TSR and adjusted FCF each decreased from one-third to 30 per cent. The extent to which GSK's CEO can realise immediate pay gains from hitting these targets is mitigated by the SOR requirements for maintaining the levels of shareholding stated earlier.

In 2011, GSK also began including innovation targets in their executive remuneration schemes. From 2011 to 2015, GSK included business diversification and R&D new product performance targets, with each accounting for 25 per cent of the PSP. In 2016, however, the business diversification target was dropped, so the remaining R&D performance target now accounted for one-third of PSP. In 2020, the R&D new product performance target was reduced to 20 per cent and renamed innovation sales. In addition, in 2020, the board added a new innovation metric to PSP called pipeline performance (PP), which can account for up to 20 per cent of total PSP awards. PP includes two equally weighted targets: one target is linked to the start of pivotal trials, mainly for candidates entering into phase III clinical trials, and the second target is linked to major regulatory approvals.

GSK's adoption of innovation metrics along with financial metrics should be viewed as an attempt by the board to influence the balance between innovation and financialisation in the company. The introduction of the SOR requirements is intended to mitigate financialisation by ensuring that senior executives accumulate shares that are multiples of their salaries before they can realise gains from them. The increased emphasis on performance pay, whether using innovation or financial metrics, is in keeping with the Combined Code, which requires companies listed on the London Stock Exchange to increase the variable portion of executive pay through LTIs. The types of metrics in LTIs, however, are up to each company, which takes into account guidelines advocated by major institutional shareholders.

It should be recognised that this complicated morass of executive pay components and their qualifications originated with a focus on stock-price performance in a financialised business model. With the attempted transition from financialisation to innovation, the board has sought to introduce into the remuneration schemes productive performance measures as well as conditionalities for realising gains from stock-based pay. In the end, however, it is our view that any senior executive who has the ability and incentive to pursue an innovation strategy should be satisfied with a reasonable salary and perhaps a bonus. In that way, senior executives can devote their energies to running an innovative enterprise, rather than be concerned with how each move they make is going to affect their pay package.

6 Explaining the Financialisation-to-Innovation Transition at AstraZeneca and GlaxoSmithKline

Our study of the operation and performance of AZN and GSK has found that both companies adopted a financialised business model in the 2000s – the first decade after the international mergers that created the two UK-based Big Pharma companies. In the following decade, however, first AZN, very decisively, and then GSK, more tentatively, made the strategic shift from financialisation to innovation. The orientation of these companies towards innovation has been sustained during the early years of the 2020s, although both remain vulnerable to pressures to revert to a financialised business model.

Given AZN's soaring stock price and high dividend payments, its shareholders have thus far been beneficiaries of this change in corporate strategy.

The company has also grown its employment from 51,600 worldwide in 2013 to 79,600 in 2021, including an increase in the UK from 7,200 to 8,900. Most importantly, AZN is now far more focused on developing safe and effective medicines than it was a decade ago. With the onset of the COVID-19 crisis, the world in general, and the UK in particular, realised the benefit of AZN's reorientation towards innovation, as the UK-based company was able and willing to cooperate with the UK government and Oxford University in developing a COVID-19 vaccine, with a no-profit pledge for delivery during the pandemic.

As we have documented, a key indicator of the strategic transition from financialisation to innovation at both AZN and GSK was the decision of their boards to cease doing open-market repurchases – aka stock buybacks. AZN stopped doing buybacks in 2013, while GSK cut them out completely from 2018. The resultant benefit to these companies was not simply, or even primarily, that it freed up funds to be reinvested in their productive capabilities. Rather, of far more importance, the cessation of buybacks manifested a recognition by those who exercise strategic control that a committed corporate focus on innovation cannot coexist with the use of corporate funds for the purpose of manipulating the company's stock price. The only beneficiaries of buybacks are stock traders who are looking for the opportunistic moment to sell the company's shares. The use of corporate funds for stock-price manipulation has no role to play in a company that is fulfilling its purpose by investing in innovation.

Recently, the importance of eschewing buybacks in making the transition from financialisation to innovation has even been recognised by the CEOs of two US-based companies – Pfizer and Intel – that had been among the most highly financialised business corporations in the United States (and, ergo, the world). In the decade 2010–19, among all US-based industrial corporations, Pfizer ranked number 7 with $76.7 billion in buybacks (60 per cent of net income, with another 56 per cent distributed as dividends), while Intel was number 9 with $66.8 billion in buybacks (51 per cent of net income, with another 36 per cent paid out as dividends). In each of the cases, the new CEO stated explicitly that he viewed stock buybacks as antithetical to innovation.

A highly financialised corporation from the late 1980s, in early 2019 Pfizer committed to doing $8.9 billion in buybacks, with $6.8 billion as an 'accelerated share repurchase' (ASR) to be completed by August of that year.[6] Thereafter,

---

6 Pfizer's broker executed $2.1 billion in open-market repurchases in the first quarter of 2019 (ending 31 March) but none thereafter. In addition, on 7 February 2019, Pfizer entered into a $6.8 billion accelerated share repurchase (ASR) agreement with Goldman Sachs. An ASR (which Pfizer had also done in February 2017 and March 2018) is a device for stock-price manipulation that enables a company to reduce its shares outstanding by the full number of

the company ceased doing buybacks as it turned its strategic attention to conserving a portion of its profits to finance investment in its drug pipeline. Previously, Pfizer's strategy had been to acquire other companies with lucrative drugs on the market that had years of patent life left and to extract the profits to fund its distributions to shareholders. Indeed, in 2014, Pfizer had attempted, but failed, to acquire AZN (AstraZeneca 2014). By 2019, however, with the patents on a number of Pfizer's major drugs expiring and even midcap pharmaceutical acquisition targets disappearing, Pfizer's board recognised that, unless it could develop high-revenue drugs internally, the company itself could become vulnerable to acquisition by another Big Pharma competitor.

From August 2019 through December 2021, for the sake of internal drug development, Pfizer did no buybacks. Indeed, in a rare move among US corporations, in January 2020 (with no premonition of the profits that it would be reaping through its collaboration with BioNTech in the delivery of a COVID-19 vaccine), Pfizer publicly announced its commitment to forego buybacks that year, and it did so again in January 2021. The company did, however, increase its dividend in 2019, 2020, and 2021.

The implementation of this change in Pfizer's investment strategy followed the end of Ian Read's tenure as Pfizer CEO as of 1 January 2019, in favour of current CEO Albert Bourla (whose background is veterinary medicine and who had been with Pfizer since 1993). As CEO from 2011, Read (an accountant by training, who had joined Pfizer in 1978) had implemented the financialisation strategy that we call 'downsize-and-distribute': the company downsized its labour force and distributed cash to shareholders in the form of dividends and buybacks (Lazonick et al. 2019).

In an earnings call with stock-market analysts in January 2020 (Pfizer 2020), Bourla made an extraordinary admission of the company's financialised past, declaring that Pfizer had stopped doing buybacks so that the company could invest in innovation:

> The reason why in our capital allocation, we are allocating right now money [is] to increase the dividend and also to invest in our business … all the CapEx to modernize our facilities. The reason why we don't do right now

---

shares in the agreement on the date on which it signs the ASR contract. This arrangement gives an immediate, that is, 'accelerated', boost to the company's earnings-per-share (EPS), without the company transgressing the daily limits for open-market repurchases under the SEC's Rule 10b-18 (see Lazonick and Jacobson 2022). The bank (in this case Goldman Sachs) borrows the shares specified in the ASR agreement from asset funds that are not seeking to sell the shares. Then, during the life of the ASR agreement, the bank purchases the company's shares on the stock market in smaller amounts at its discretion at various points in time and returns the borrowed shares to the asset funds. In the case of Pfizer's 2019 ASR, Goldman Sachs completed it in August 2019.

share repurchases, it is because we want to make sure that we maintain very strong firepower to invest in the business. The past was a very different Pfizer. The past of the last decade had to deal with declining of revenues, constant declining of revenues. And we had to do what we had to do even if that was financial engineering, purchasing back ourselves. We couldn't invest them and create higher value. Now it's a very different situation. We are a very different company.

Bourla did not explain why the 'old' Pfizer – which, less than twelve months before, had done $8.9 billion in buybacks – 'had to do what we had to do even if that was financial engineering, purchasing back ourselves.' But his rambling statement is a very rare recognition by a CEO of a major US corporation that stock buybacks are the enemy of investment in innovation. In the event, however, with Pfizer's revenue bonanza from its COVID-19 vaccine and pill, the company is flush with cash, and in the first quarter of 2022 not only raised its dividends again but also did $2.0 billion of stock buybacks to help increase its stock price.

As the case of Pfizer clearly illustrates, and as shown in our studies of AZN and GSK, even within business corporations that have become the leading repurchasers of their own stock, there is an ongoing tension between innovation and financialisation, with the outcomes determined by specific sets of circumstances related to technologies, markets, and competition. In the semiconductor industry – which has an R&D intensity on a par with pharmaceuticals – Intel offers another example of a shift in corporate strategy from financialisation to innovation, with cessation of buybacks as an important part of that intended transformation.

Once the world leader in chip fabrication, a financialised Intel found itself falling behind in the face of innovative global competition. Under new leadership, however, Intel is now seeking to invest in advanced nanometer fabrication facilities with the goal of catching up with industry frontrunners TSMC and Samsung Electronics (Lazonick and Hopkins 2021a). Intel ceased doing stock buybacks from the second quarter of 2021 after replacing CEO Robert Swan, a finance expert, with Pat Gelsinger, a technology expert (Lazonick and Hopkins 2021b). In May 2021, in a television interview on the popular *60 Minutes* show, Gelsinger said that a condition of his taking the top Intel job was assurances from the company's board that Intel would 'not be anywhere near as focused on buybacks going forward as we have in the past' (Stahl 2021).

In a subsequent interview with *CNET* in November 2021, Gelsinger was much more expansive and emphatic (CNET 2021). He recounted how, before taking the CEO job, he had written a strategy paper for Intel's board, for which he got their unanimous agreement. 'I was concerned', Gelsinger said in the interview, 'about how we get the process roadmap back in shape'. He continued:

> We underinvested in capital. I went to the board and said: 'We're done with buybacks. We are investing in factories. And that is going to be the use of our cash as we go forward.' And they aggressively supported that perspective; that we needed to just start investing, and those investments would start creating a cycle of momentum that would get our factory teams executing better.

Among US-based business corporations, these two recent cases of rejection of buybacks for the sake of investing in innovation are exceptions (and, as we have just seen, at Pfizer ephemeral). US-based companies began doing large-scale open-market repurchases in 1984, after the US SEC, by adopting Rule 10b-18 in November 1982, had in effect legalised the use of open-market repurchases by a company to manipulate its own stock price. The 216 companies in the S&P 500 Index in January 2020 listed continuously on the stock market from 1981 through 2019 distributed 49.7 per cent of their net income as dividends and just 4.4 per cent as buybacks in 1981–83, whereas the same 216 companies distributed 49.6 per cent as dividends and 62.2 per cent as buybacks in 2017–19 (Lazonick, 2022a).

In 2018, all 500 companies in the S&P 500 Index did a then-record $806 billion in buybacks, with their profits inflated by the Republican-supported Tax Cuts and Jobs Act of 2017. This legislation drastically cut the corporate tax rate on current profits as well as on those past profits that US-based corporations held abroad, on which taxes would only be collected upon repatriation (Lazonick et al. 2020). In arguing against these tax cuts, many Congressional Democrats were vocal critics of the stock buybacks that the augmented corporate profits would fund. Yet in 2021 with Democrats controlling the House, Senate, and Presidency, the 2018 buyback record was eclipsed as S&P 500 companies did $882 billion in share repurchases (Pisani 2021; Lazonick 2022a).

Indeed, when he was vice-president of the United States, Joe Biden published an opinion piece in the *Wall Street Journal*, in which he argued that buybacks, incentivised by stock-based executive pay, posed a major obstacle to achieving stable and equitable growth in the US economy (Biden 2016; Lazonick 2022a). This view of the deleterious impacts of buybacks on industrial innovation and income distribution in the United States finds empirical support in a growing body of research, much of it carried out by the Academic-Industry Research Network (with which the three authors of this Element are associated) and funded by the Institute for New Economic Thinking (Lazonick 2022a). As we have done in this Element for the cases of AZN and GSK, the evidence for the value destruction wrought by corporate financialisation derives from the study of particular companies, including Apple, Boeing, Cisco, Exxon Mobil, General Electric, General Motors, Gilead Sciences, Hewlett-Packard, IBM, Intel, McDonald's, Merck, Microsoft, Motorola, and Pfizer (Lazonick 2022a).

In *Predatory Value Extraction: How the Looting of the Business Corporation Became the US Norm and How Sustainable Prosperity Can Be Restore*d, William Lazonick and Jang-Sup Shin provide an analysis of how the orientation of the US corporation towards value extraction at the expense of value creation involves the tripartite interaction of corporate managers as value-extracting 'insiders', asset managers as value-extracting 'enablers', and hedge-fund managers as value-extracting 'outsiders'. US-style stock-based pay incentivises senior executives as insiders to do buybacks to boost the company's stock price, rewarding them with inflated realised gains on their stock-based pay. In the process, since the 1980s, corporate executives have embraced the destructive ideology that a company should be run to 'maximize shareholder value' (MSV). Meanwhile, US government policy, put in place from the late 1980s to the early 2000s, has greatly enhanced the value-extracting power of hedge-fund managers, as outsiders, to secure portfolio investments and proxy votes from asset managers, as enablers, to put pressure on corporate managers, as insiders, to distribute corporate cash to shareholders.

As a result of this interaction, a corporate predator such as William Ackman, Carl Icahn, Daniel Loeb, Nelson Peltz, or Paul Singer – to name some of the most prominent 'hedge-fund activists' – who purchase a shareholding stake of, say, 1 per cent of a company on the stock market can mobilise sufficient proxy votes from institutional investors to credibly threaten incumbent corporate management with ouster unless they increase their distributions of buybacks and dividends. The value-extracting outsiders demand that, by price-gouging customers, laying off employees, suppressing wages and benefits, squeezing suppliers and distributors, divesting corporate assets, taking on debt, depleting the corporate treasury, and avoiding corporate taxes, the value-extracting insiders can augment the so-called 'free' cash flow that can 'create value' for shareholders. In the 1980s and 1990s, insiders often viewed this type of outsider pressure as 'hostile', but in the twenty-first-century US corporate economy the overt hostility has disappeared as collaboration between the insiders and outsiders in predatory value extraction has become the business norm (Lazonick and Shin 2020; Lazonick 2022a).

In principle, a pension fund or mutual fund that does not churn its stock portfolio should favour distributions as dividends, while leaving the company with sufficient retentions to provide a financial foundation for investment in innovation. If these investments in productive capabilities are well managed, higher future revenues and profits should lead to an increase in the company's future stock price, so that the asset fund can realise a gain of any shares that it may decide to sell. In the United States, however, asset-fund managers, in search of the higher quarterly yields on their portfolios needed to keep their jobs, often invest some of their funds with, and provide their proxy votes to, hedge-fund activists engaged in predatory value extraction.

This interaction among value-extracting insiders, enablers, and outsiders explains the fact that over the past two decades, especially when the stock market is rising, buybacks have far surpassed dividends as a form of distribution of corporate cash to shareholders in the United States. In contrast, despite the contagion, via business schools and board rooms, of predatory MSV ideology from the United States to the United Kingdom since the late 1980s, UK institutional arrangements, as in Europe more generally, favour realising gains from 'shareholding' rather than 'shareselling'. Research by our colleague Mustafa Erdem Sakınç (2017) on corporate value extraction in the United States (S&P 500 companies) and Europe (S&P Europe 350 companies) for 2000 to 2015 shows that (a) in contrast to the United States, dividends have been substantially higher than buybacks in Europe, including the United Kingdom, and (b) while buybacks increased in Europe, including the United Kingdom, during the 2000s before declining sharply in the 2009 financial crisis, their increase after the financial crisis was modest, especially when compared with the boom in buybacks that occurred in the first half of the 2010s (and beyond) in the United States.

In the United Kingdom, corporate-governance recommendations of the Cadbury (1992), Greenbury (1995), and Hampel (1998) reports, that formed the basis for the 'Combined Code', functioned in effect as the British business community's defence of 'shareholder primacy' against the unconstrained ideology of predatory value extraction being transmitted by MSV ideologues from the United States to the United Kingdom. The *UK Corporate Governance Code* promulgated by the Financial Reporting Council (2018) continues to help insulate UK-based business corporations from the US system of predatory value extraction, providing a distinctive institutional environment in which both the onset of financialisation and the subsequent transition from financialisation to innovation at AZN and GSK can be understood.[7]

Our detailed analysis of what actually occurred at AZN and GSK since the mergers that created them permits us to provide answers to the following questions: (i) why did the two companies become financialised during the first

---

[7] For an earlier study of the tension between innovation and financialisation at a major UK-based corporation, see Lazonick and Prencipe (2005).

decade of their existence? (ii) when and why did these companies make the transition from financialisation to innovation over the past decade? (iii) going forward, how sustainable is AZN's and GSK's commitment to innovation and resistance to financialisation?

The impetus to financialisation at AZN and GSK was inherent in the international consolidations that created the two corporations at the end of the 1990s. It was a period in which stock markets were booming, with Europeans becoming enamoured with the apparent success of the US New Economy business model in supporting high-tech start-ups in information-and-communication technology and biotech. Established Old Economy corporations executed buybacks to give manipulative boosts to their stock prices to keep pace with the valuations of leading New Economy companies, whose stock-price increases were driven by a combination of innovation and speculation. When an international merger occurred, there was a focus on what it would mean for the new company's stock price and how it might be supported.

In the merger that created AZN, the involvement of Investor AB, the long-standing industrial foundation of the Wallenberg family, held out the potential for a company that was much less financialised than AZN in fact would become in the 2000s. Investor's general orientation was what we call 'retain-and-reinvest': it retained corporate profits within the industrial companies in which it held large stakes (typically reinforced by voting power from dual-class shares) and reinvested in productive capabilities (see, e.g., Glimstedt et al. 2006). In the 'merger of equals' that created AZN, however, Investor had to share power; the directorships were split evenly between Astra and Zeneca, with the UK-based company securing four out of seven non-executive positions, including that of the CEO McKillop.

At the outset, Investor was one of the largest shareholders at AZN with direct ownership of 5.2 per cent, but it reduced its shareholding to 3.9 per cent in 2005 to take advantage of a high stock price to sell AZN shares to help fund its purchase of Scania shares. In addition, there were a number of other Swedish institutional shareholders connected to the Wallenbergs, with a combined 21 per cent, who could be counted upon to support Investor's governance position. Apparently, however, more influential than Investor and its Swedish allies as an AZN's shareholder after the merger was US-based Capital Group with a holding of 7.8 per cent, which it increased to a peak of 15.0 per cent in 2004. Throughout the period 2000–7, with AZN's shares trading on NYSE as American Depository Receipts (ADRs), the pattern of

AZN's buybacks resembled those of US-based companies, more than tripling from £620 million in 2003 to £2.1 billion in 2006 and remaining at that level in 2007.

In 2006, AZN appointed Brennan as the new CEO to replace McKillop. He had come from Zeneca to be head of AZN's US operations, and his elevation to the company's top executive position served to reinforce AZN's MSV orientation. Even though AZN's profits increased substantially in 2008–9, the company reduced its buybacks sharply, doing none in 2009, as was the case for most S&P 500 companies in the United States. Meanwhile, Capital Group reduced its AZN shareholding from 11.7 per cent in 2007 to 4.9 per cent in 2008 and held around 3 per cent from 2010 through 2017.

It was not only buybacks that were draining cash from AZN. Under Brennan, AZN increased its dividends from annual averages of £1.2 billion in 2006–7 to £1.9 billion in 2008–9 and £2.4 billion in 2010–12, when dividends absorbed 44 per cent of net income. The company also resumed its buybacks in 2010–12, spending another 46 per cent of net income. In 2011, when AZN's profits shot up to a record £6.4 billion, buybacks were £3.9 billion. But in 2012, AZN faced a dramatic loss of revenues as patents expired on its blockbuster drugs. Its profits fell to £3.9 billion in 2012, virtually the exact same amount that the company had wasted on buybacks the previous year. Brennan and his financialised strategy had reached the end of the line.

As we have seen, in the period 1999–2012, AZN became highly financialised notwithstanding the presence of the 'patient capitalist' Investor AB representatives, including Marcus Wallenberg, on its board and as an influential major shareholder. In the case of the merger that created GSK, the UK-based Glaxo Wellcome combined with the US-based SKB, which was much more directly exposed to the MSV corporate-governance ideology emanating from US business schools and board rooms. Despite the fact that the vast majority of GSK shareholders were British, after the merger the administrative headquarters of the UK-based company were in Philadelphia, where SmithKline had originated. As GSK's first CEO, Garnier, who had joined SmithKline in 1990 and had become the chief operating officer of SKB in 1995, insisted on continuing to work from the Philadelphia base.

From 2000 to 2012, the pattern of buybacks and dividends at GSK was very similar to that at AZN, with GSK's buybacks almost quadrupling from £980 million in 2003 to £3.8 billion in 2007 (see Appendix 1). Indeed, despite the fact that most major companies sharply reduced buybacks in 2008, GSK again executed £3.8 billion in that year. In ramping up its buybacks in 2007 and 2008, GSK was attempting to reverse the decline in its stock price, precipitated by first, in May 2007, a study that linked its Avandia drug to cardiovascular events and, then, in July 2008, a US FDA ruling that GSK had to include a 'black box' warning in dispensing the medicine.

It would appear that, by boosting the company's stock price, a portion of these buybacks helped to inflate Garnier's take-home pay, as he cashed in on stock awards around his retirement in May 2008. A public outcry against Garnier's 'overgenerous US-style pay' package in 2003 had been one of the first cases of the implementation of the UK 'say on pay' policy, which gives shareholders the right to vote on whether an executive's remuneration is excessive (Timmons 2003). In the wake of the financial crisis, the US Dodd-Frank Act of 2010 included a 'say on pay' mandate, borrowing the policy that the UK had earlier implemented to contain the contagion in UK-based companies from US-style stock-based pay.

From 2000 to 2008, GSK's outstanding debt quadrupled from £4.0 billion to £16.2 billion, with much of it being used to finance buybacks and dividends (GSK 2007, pp. 40 and 48; 2008, pp. 47 and 57). In 2007–8 alone, GSK increased its debt load by £10.7 billion while doing £7.5 billion in buybacks along with dividends of £5.7 billion. In 2009–10, after Witty took over as CEO, the company reduced buybacks to just tens of millions of pounds, although dividends were increased. Large-scale buybacks resumed in 2011–12, with an annual average of £2.4 billion, before being cut to £1.5 billion in 2013, £333 million in 2014, and an annual average of £79 million in 2015–17. Meanwhile GSK increased its dividends from £3.0 billion in 2009 to a peak of £4.9 billion in 2016, even though its profits were £5.5 billion in 2009 and only £912 million in 2016. GSK may have paid this enormous 2016 dividend based on its net income of £8.4 billion in 2015. However, £7.7 billion of that was extraordinary net income from asset exchanges with Novartis. While ramping up dividends, GSK dramatically reduced buybacks during Witty's last four years of 2014–17, not because of a strategic transition from financialisation to innovation, as occurred from 2013 at AZN, but rather because of the exceedingly low profit margins that resulted from Witty's strategy of mass-producing commodity medicines and the company policy of paying more dividends.

When and Why did AZN and GSK Begin the Transition from Financialisation to Innovation?

By 2012, AZN had become thoroughly financialised. It also had accumulated substantial debt, although most of it was because of the high cost of its MedImmune acquisition in 2007. There had been intense competition among Big Pharma companies for immunotherapies, but in the case of MedImmune its price tag was inflated by a 21 per cent premium because hedge-fund predator

Carl Icahn has bought shares in the company to force it to sell itself. In the event, whereas GSK had loaded itself with debt to do buybacks, at least AZN had in its possession a potentially valuable biologics company based in the United States. Similarly, in December 2020, Paul Singer of Elliott Management forced US-based Alexion to sell itself, with AZN acquiring the company at a 45 per cent premium. This acquisition was made in stock and cash, with a part of the payment funded by long-term debt.

In 2012, during the UK movement that became known as 'shareholders' spring', AZN shareholders rejected Brennan's proposed pay package, leading him to step down as CEO on 31 May 2012. On 1 June, Leif Johansson, the chairman of Sweden-based Ericsson, a company controlled by Investor AB, became non-executive chairman of AZN. Wallenberg, who had remained on AZN's board since the 1999 merger, led the search for a new CEO who would rebuild AZN's capabilities through internal drug development. In this campaign, Wallenberg received the support of Woodford, the highly visible fund manager at Invesco Perpetual, which held 5.7 per cent of AZN shares, while Investor AB held 4.1 per cent. In October 2012, AZN appointed Soriot as CEO. In 2009–10 he had been the CEO of Genentech, the wholly owned US-based division of Roche and, then, became the chief operating officer of Roche's pharmaceutical division. As the world's most innovative immunotherapy company, Roche with its Genentech division has been a training ground for executives like Soriot who have the capability to engage in drug innovation.

Given the precarious financial position of AZN upon Soriot's arrival, followed by the attempted takeover of AZN by Pfizer in 2013–14, the path to innovation was even more uncertain than would generally be the case in the pharmaceutical industry. AZN's board has kept shareholders happy and the stock price high by paying ample dividends. But, as we have seen, the company ceased doing buybacks entirely, with zero done from 2013 through 2021.

In contrast, in 2017, when Witty retired as CEO, a transition to innovation at GSK had not yet taken place. Moreover, unlike Soriot at AZN, the new GSK CEO, Walmsley, had no experience in leading drug development. She had come to GSK from L'Oreal in 2010 to lead the consumer health business. Besides the desire of the GSK board to appoint a female CEO, Walmsley was chosen because of the plan of demerger of the consumer health business. As CEO, however, Walmsley began the transition from financialisation to innovation by hiring a strong R&D team led by Hal Barron, who among other positions had been the chief medical officer at Genentech. Under Barron, GSK's focus shifted away from mass-produced commodity drugs to highly specialised oncology drugs. Since Walmsley became CEO, GSK has not done any buybacks.

Between 2018 and 2021, the average dividend was £4.0 billion, even after spinning off the consumer health division.

How Sustainable are AZN's and GSK's Commitments to Innovation and Resistance to Financialisation?

As of this writing in May 2022, there is no sign that AZN has lost its commitment to innovation. In Soriot's first full year as CEO in 2013, AZN annual revenues fell from $28.0 billion to $25.7 billion. In the context of AZN's rejection in May 2014 of Pfizer's takeover attempt, Soriot pledged to increase AZN revenue to $45 billion by 2023, at which point he would have served a decade as CEO. In 2021, AZN revenues were $37.4 billion, up from $26.6 billion a year earlier, with $3.7 billion in new revenues from Alexion's products and $3.9 billion from the COVID-19 vaccine. The key question concerning AZN's commitment to innovation is the possibility of Soriot's retirement in the upcoming years. Although some shareholders have criticised Soriot's remuneration package, the innovation regime he has put in place at AZN has been widely lauded. The one potential weakness in sustaining the company's commitment to innovation is AZN's high level of indebtedness combined with a high dividend policy in an industry in which future product revenues face technological, market and competitive uncertainty.

As for GSK, the shift from financialisation to innovation is half a decade behind that of AZN, and the company was much less endowed with productive capabilities than its UK-based competitor to make that transition. GSK's failure to develop a COVID-19 vaccine in collaboration with France-based Sanofi was a sign of weakness in the innovative capabilities in one of its legacy businesses. As Walmsley sought to build GSK's oncology capabilities, the company was attacked in 2021 by US corporate predator Singer of Elliott Management, who demanded that Walmsley step down as GSK's CEO to become the head of the consumer health division that was in the process of being spun off as an independent company in a joint venture with Pfizer. Walmsley, however, insisted that she would remain CEO of GSK, and the board backed her up. If anything, her success in standing up to one of the world's most notorious 'vulture capitalists' strengthened her position at the head of GSK.

A potential weakness that Walmsley faces is a lack of commitment of the leadership of the R&D team she has put in place to implement the company's innovation strategy. In January 2022, Barron abruptly announced that he was leaving his position as head of the R&D team to join a Silicon Valley biotech start-up called Altos Labs as CEO. In April 2022, organisational disruption came from UK employees who staged strikes because their pay increases in 2021 had failed to keep pace with inflation (Reuters Staff 2022). Like AZN, GSK has significant long-term debt and is committed to a high dividend policy, both of which could impede its financial commitment to innovative products.

Sustaining an innovation trajectory requires above all that those executives who exercise strategic control possess the abilities and incentives to invest corporate resources in a process that is uncertain, collective and cumulative. The only way to overcome the uncertainty inherent in drug innovation is to integrate the company's employees into collective learning processes. Without organisational learning, innovation cannot occur. Strategies for maintaining the continuous employment of labour engaged in organisational learning should be a top priority of government policy to support innovative enterprises and their ecosystems, as stressed by Sainsbury (2020). To sustain this learning process requires financial commitment which, for both AZN and GSK, would pose a potential problem should revenues and profits decline, especially if levels of indebtedness are high or increasing.

What should occur under such circumstances is a reduction in dividend payments for the sake of sustaining the innovation process and regenerating the revenue and profit streams. It is well known, however, that whether in the United States or United Kingdom, companies are reluctant to cut dividends. In essence, for both individual and institutional shareholders, dividends in an established corporation are seen as an 'entitlement'. If, however, a company wants to maintain its investment in innovation in the face of financial constraints, the funding should be secured by cutting dividends, not the labour force.

From the perspective of the theory of innovative enterprise, which has provided the conceptual framework for these studies of AZN and GSK, UK government policy should focus on strengthening corporate governance institutions that promote 'retain-and-reinvest' and constrain 'downsize-and-distribute'; structuring employment institutions that can prepare the labour force for the learning challenges of the twenty-first century and provide opportunities for engaging in this learning in the United Kingdom; and implementing tax policy and other financial incentives to reinforce financial commitment by those companies that seek to invest in innovation in the United Kingdom.

It has long been claimed that capitalism is an engine of innovation. Reinventing capitalism for the sake of stable and equitable economic growth means eliminating value destruction caused by financialisation and supporting value creation through collective and cumulative innovation.

Appendix

Appendix 1 Sources and uses of funds at AZN and GSK (£2021 billion), 2002–21

AstraZeneca (£2021 billion)

	Sources of funds (SF)					Distributions to shareholders (DS)		Cash investments in productive capabilities (CIPC)			Totals		
	REV	NI	Adjust.	TDBT, ΔYTY	CCE	BB	DV	RD	CAPEX	Cash Acq.	SF	DS	CIPC
2002–2006	86	16	5	(0)	14	9	6	14	4	1	21	15	19
2007–2011	126	29	9	7	30	10	12	20	4	10	46	22	34
2012–2016	96	12	12	9	26	2	13	21	4	10	33	15	35
2017–2021	103	8	16	9	21	0	14	24	4	3	33	14	31
2002–2011	212	45	14	7	44	19	18	34	8	11	67	37	53
2012–2021	198	20	27	18	47	2	27	44	8	13	65	29	66

GSK (£2021 billion)

	Sources of funds (SF)					Distributions to shareholders (DS)		Cash investments in productive capabilities (CIPC)			Totals		
	REV	NI	Adjust.	TDBT, ΔYTY	CCE	BB	DV	RD	CAPEX	Cash Acq.	SF	DS	CIPC
2002–2006	154	32	8	2	17	9	17	22	7	3	42	27	31
2007–2011	166	28	11	12	34	13	19	23	8	6	52	32	37
2012–2016	144	25	12	4	28	5	23	19	7	7	41	28	33
2017–2021	169	21	15	6	24	0	21	22	7	1	41	21	30
2002–2011	320	61	19	14	51	22	37	44	15	9	94	59	68
2012–2021	313	46	27	10	52	5	43	42	14	8	83	48	63

Notes: Acquisitions-Cash [ACQ-CSH]; Adjustment = Depreciations + Amortisation (of goodwill and intangible fixed assets) + Impairment (and assets written off); Year-to-Year Change [ΔYTY] in Total Debt [TDBT]; Cash and Cash equivalents [CCE]; GSK-CCE= Bank balances and deposits + US treasury and treasury repo only money market funds + liquid funds.
Sources: Authors' calculations based on S&P Capital IQ.

References

Andreoni, A., 2018. 'The architecture and dynamics of industrial ecosystems', *Cambridge Journal of Economics*, 42, 6: 1613–42.

Andreoni, A., and Lazonick, W., 2020. 'Local ecosystems and social conditions of innovative enterprise', in Oqubay, A., and Lin, J., eds., *The Oxford Handbook of Industrial Hubs and Economic Development*, Oxford: Oxford University Press: 77–97.

AstraZeneca, 2004. Form-20 F published on 21 March 2005, https://www.astrazeneca.com/content/dam/az/Investor_Relations/annual-reports-home page/2004-Annual-Report-English.pdf.

AstraZeneca, 2014. 'AstraZeneca board rejects Pfizer's final proposal', AstraZeneca Press Release, 19 May, https://www.astrazeneca.com/media-centre/press-releases/2014/astrazeneca-board-rejects-pfizers-final-proposal-19052014.html#.

AstraZeneca, 2021. 'AstraZeneca in the United Kingdom', AstraZeneca, https://careers.astrazeneca.com/united-kingdom.

Baldwin, C., and Clark, K., 1992. 'Capabilities and capital investment: New perspectives on capital budgeting', *Journal of Applied Corporate Finance*, 5, 2: 67–87.

Barriaux, M., 2007. 'Shareholders attack AstraZeneca's acquisition', *Guardian*, 27 April, www.theguardian.com/business/2007/apr/27/10.

Batiz-Lazo, B., 2004. *GlaxoSmithKline: A Merger Too Far?* (No. 0405003). University Library of Munich, Germany.

BEIS, 2017. 'Industrial strategy: Life sciences sector deal', UK Department for Business, Energy & Industrial Strategy, 6 December, https://assets.publishing.service.gov.uk/government/uploads/system/uploads/attachment_data/file/665452/life-sciences-sector-deal-web-ready-version.pdf.

BEIS, 2021. 'Build back better: Our plan for growth – Life sciences vision', UK Department for Business, Energy & Industrial Strategy, 6 July 2021, https://www.gov.uk/government/publications/build-back-better-our-plan-for-growth.

Biden, J., 2016. 'How short-termism saps the economy', *Wall Street Journal*, 27 September, www.wsj.com/articles/how-short-termism-saps-the-economy-1475018087.

Binder, G., and Bashe, P., 2008. *Science Lessons: What the Business of Biotech Taught Me about Management*. Harvard Business School Press: Boston.

Birkett, K., 2001. *Inside The Glaxo Wellcome and SmithKline Merger*. Legal & Commercial: London.

Bradshaw, J., 2018. 'GSK chief denies pressure to split company', *Telegraph*, 22 December, www.telegraph.co.uk/business/2018/12/22/gsk-chief-denies-pressure-split-company/.

Brown-Humes, C., 2004. 'Investor sells $1bn stake in AstraZeneca', *Financial Times,* 11 February.

Burgess, K., and McCrum, D., 2012. 'Boards wake up to a shareholder spring', *Financial Times,* 4 May, https://www.ft.com/content/a284e414-95ee-11e1-a163-00144feab49a.

Cadbury Report, 1992. *Report of the Committee on the Financial Aspects of Corporate Governance*. Gee: London, 1 December, https://ecgi.global/sites/default/files//codes/documents/cadbury.pdf.

Carpenter, M., and Lazonick, W., 2017. 'Innovation, competition, and financialization in the communications technology industry', ISIGrowth Working Paper No. 8, May 2017, www.isigrowth.eu/2017/06/14/innovation-competition-and-financialization-in-the-communications-technology-industry-1996-2016/.

Chang, H.-J., and Andreoni, A., 2020. 'Industrial policy in the 21st century', *Development and Change*, 51, 2: 324–51.

Christensen, C. M., Kaufman, S. P., and Shih, W. C., 2008. 'Innovation killers: How financial tools destroy your capacity to do new things', *Harvard Business Review*, 86, 1: 98–105.

CNET, 2021. 'Intel CEO Pat Gelsinger! (CNET's full interview)', *CNET Highlights*, 19 November, www.youtube.com/watch?v=_y-GWcsK6Ag&t=5s.

Collington, R., and Lazonick, W., 2022. 'Pricing for medicine innovation: A regulatory approach for supporting drug development and patient access', Institute for New Economic Thinking Working Paper No. 176, 28 January, https://www.ineteconomics.org/research/research-papers/pricing-for-medicine-innovation-a-regulatory-approach-to-support-drug-development-and-patient-access.

Cook, D., Brown, D., Alexander, R. et al., 2014. 'Lessons learned from the fate of AstraZeneca's drug pipeline: A five-dimensional framework', *Nature Reviews Drug Discovery*, 13, 6: 419–31.

Corley, T., 2010. 'Twentieth-century American contributions to the growth of the Beecham enterprise', in Quirke, V. and Slinn, J. eds., *Perspectives on Twentieth-Century Pharmaceuticals*, Peter Lang: Oxford: 217–40.

Crystal, G., 1991. *In Search of Excess: The Overcompensation of American Executives*. W. W. Norton & Company: New York.

De La Merced, M., 2017. 'Elliott management is said push for changes at Alexion', *New York Times*, 7 December, https://www.nytimes.com/2017/12/07/business/dealbook/elliott-alexion-activist-investor.html.

Evans, R., 2014. 'Neil Woodford: Pfizer has clearly recognised that AstraZeneca has changed massively for the better'. *The Telegraph*, 3 May.

Financial Reporting Council, 2018. The UK corporate governance code, July, https://www.frc.org.uk/getattachment/88bd8c45-50ea-4841-95b0-d2f4f48069a2/2018-uk-corporate-governance-code-final.pdf.

Froud, J., Johal, S., Leaver, A., and Williams, K., 2006. *Financialization and Strategy: Narrative and Numbers*. Routledge: London.

Fry, E., and Zillman, C., 2018. 'Science "mojo" and an executive dream team: CEO Emma Walmsley's bold prescription for reviving GlaxoSmithKline', *Fortune,* 28 September, https://fortune.com/longform/gsk-glaxosmithkline-ceo-emma-walmsley/.

Gagnon, M., and Volesky, K., 2017. 'Merger mania: Mergers and acquisitions in the generic drug sector from 1995 to 2016', *Globalization and Health*, 13, 62: 1–7.

Gleadle, P., Parris, S., Shipman, A., and Simonetti, R., 2014. 'Restructuring and innovation in pharmaceuticals and biotechs: The impact of financialisation', *Critical Perspectives on Accounting*, 25, 1: 67–77.

Glimstedt, H., Lazonick, W., and Xie, H., 2006. 'Evolution and allocation of stock options: Adapting US-style compensation to the Swedish business model', *European Management Review*, 3, 3: 1–21.

Greenbury Report, 1995. *Report on Directors' Remuneration*. Gee: London, 17 July.

Griffiths, I., 1996. 'Zeneca bidders may as well stay in bed', *Independent on Sunday*, 27 October: 2, https://www.independent.co.uk/news/business/zeneca-bidders-may-as-well-stay-in-bed-1360362.html.

GSK, 2002. Form 20-F published on 28 March 2003.

GSK, 2007. Form 20-F, published on 29 February 2008, at https://www.gsk.com/media/8057/20-f-2007.pdf.

GSK, 2008 Form 20-F, published on 4 March 2009, https://www.gsk.com/media/8061/20-f-2008.pdf.

GSK, 2021. 'United Kingdom locations', GSK, https://www.gsk.com/en-gb/locations/united-kingdom/.

Gupta, H., Kumar, S. Roy, S., and Gaud, R., 2010. 'Patent protection strategies', *Journal of Pharmacy and Bioallied Sciences*, 2, 1: 2–7.

Hamilton, D., 2007. 'Icahn scores lucrative victory in MedImmune sale', *Reuters*, 23 April, www.reuters.com/article/businesspro-icahn-medimmunedc/icahn-scores-lucrative-victory-in-medimmune-sale-idUSN2329630820070423.

Hampel Report 2008. *The Hampel Report. Committee on Corporate Governance: Final Report*, Gee: London, January 1998, https://ecgi.global/code/hampel-report-final.

Haslam, C., Tsitsianis, N., Andersson, T., and Yin, Y., 2013. *Redefining Business Models: Strategies for a Financialized World*. Routledge: London.

Heracleous, L., and Murray, J., 2001. 'The urge to merge in the pharmaceutical industry', *European Management Journal*, 19, 4: 430–7.

Hirschler, B., 2007. 'AstraZeneca finance chief to join Goldman Sachs', *Reuters*, 6 June, https://www.reuters.com/article/idUSWLA971220070606.

Hirschler, B., 2016. 'GSK break-up? Don't bank on it, says drugmaker's outgoing boss', *Reuters*, 17 March, www.reuters.com/article/us-gsk-move swittygsk/gsk-break-up-dont-bank-on-it-says-drugmakers-outgoing-bossidUSKCN0WJ20E.

Hirschler, B., 2017. 'GSK may bid for Pfizer consumer unit, stoking dividend fears', *Reuters*, 25 October, www.reuters.com/article/us-gsk-results/gskmay-bid-for-pfizer-consumer-unit-stoking-dividend-fears-idUSKBN1CU1HF.

Hopkins, M., and Lazonick, W., 2016. 'The mismeasure of mammon: Uses and abuses of executive pay data', Institute for New Economic Thinking Working Paper No. 49, 12 October, https://www.ineteconomics.org/research/research-papers/the-mismeasure-of-mammon-uses-and-abuses-of-executive-pay-data.

Jacobson, K., and Lazonick, W., 2022. 'A license to loot: SEC Rule 10b-18 and alternative views of capital formation', *The Academic-Industry Research Network*, forthcoming,

Jensen, M., 1986. 'Agency costs of free cash flow, corporate finance, and takeovers', *American Economic Review*, 76, 2: 323–9.

Jensen, M., and Murphy, K., 1990. 'Performance pay and top management incentives', *Journal of Political Economy*, 98, 2: 225–64.

Jones, E., 2007. *The Business of Medicine*. B. Jain: New Delhi.

Kolhatkar, S., 2018. 'Paul Singer, doomsday investor', *New Yorker*, 20 August, www.newyorker.com/magazine/2018/08/27/paul-singer-doomsday-investor.

Kollewe, J., 2012. 'AstraZeneca boss David Brennan quits under pressure from investors', *Guardian*, 26 April, https://www.theguardian.com/business/2012/apr/26/astrazeneca-boss-quits-boardroom-coup.

Lazonick, W. 2009. *Sustainable Prosperity in the New Economy? Business Organization and High-Tech Employment in the United States*. Upjohn Institute for Employment Research, Kalamazoo, Michigan USA.

Lazonick, W., 2014a. 'Profits without prosperity: Stock buybacks manipulate the market and leave most Americans worse off', *Harvard Business Review*, September, https://hbr.org/2014/09/profits-without-prosperity.

Lazonick, W., 2014b. 'Taking stock: Why executive pay results in an unstable and inequitable economy', Roosevelt Institute White Paper, 5 June, https://www.scribd.com/document/228174585/Taking-Stock-Why-Executive-Pay-Results-in-an-Unstable-and-Inequitable-Economy.

Lazonick, W., 2015. 'Stock buybacks: From retain-and-reinvest to downsize-and-distribute', Brookings Institution, April, www.brookings.edu/research/papers/2015/04/17-stock-buybacks-lazonick.

Lazonick, W., 2018. 'The functions of the stock market and the fallacies of shareholder value', in Driver, C., and Thompson, G, eds., *What Next for Corporate Governance?* Oxford University Press: Oxford: 117–51.

Lazonick, W., 2019a. 'The theory of innovative enterprise: Foundations of economic analysis', in Clarke, T., O'Brien, J., and O'Kelley, C., eds., *The Oxford Handbook of the Corporation*, Oxford University Press: London: 490–514, https://doi.org/10.1093/oxfordhb/9780198737063.013.12.

Lazonick, W., 2019b. 'The value-extracting CEO: How executive stock-based pay undermines investment in productive capabilities', *Structural Change and Economic Dynamics*, 48: 53–68.

Lazonick, W., 2022a. 'Investing in innovation: Confronting predatory value extraction in the U.S. corporation,' Academic-Industry Research Network Working Paper 22-09/01, 26 September, https://theairnet.org/melseerg/2022/10/Lazonick-Investing-in-Innovation-20220926.pdf.

Lazonick, W., 2022b. 'Is the most unproductive firm the foundation of the most efficient economy? Penrosian learning confronts the neoclassical fallacy', *International Review of Applied Economics*, 36, 2: 1–32.

Lazonick, W., and Hopkins, M., 2016. 'If the SEC measured CEO pay packages properly, they would look even more outrageous', *Harvard Business Review*, 22 December, https://hbr.org/2016/12/if-the-sec-measured-ceo-pay-packages-properly-they-would-look-even-more-outrageous.

Lazonick, W., and Hopkins, M., 2021a. 'How Intel financialized and lost leadership in semiconductor fabrication', Institute for New Economic Thinking, 7 July, https://www.ineteconomics.org/perspectives/blog/how-intel-financialized-and-lost-leadership-in-semiconductor-fabrication.

Lazonick, W., and Hopkins, M., 2021b. 'Why the CHIPS are down: Stock buybacks and subsidies in the U.S. semiconductor industry', Institute for New Economic Thinking Working Paper No. 165, November, https://www.ineteconomics.org/research/research-papers/why-the-chips-are-down-stock-buybacks-and-subsidies-in-the-u-s-semiconductor-industry.

Lazonick, W., and Jacobson, K., 2022. 'Letter to SEC: Stock buybacks undermine investment in innovation for the sake of stock-price manipulation', Institute for New. Economic Thinking, 1 April, https://www.ineteconomics .org/perspectives/blog/letter-to-sec-a-policy-framework-for-attaining-sus tainable-prosperity-in-the-united-states.

Lazonick, W., and Prencipe, A., 2005. 'Dynamic capabilities and sustained innovation: Strategic control and financial commitment at Rolls-Royce plc', *Industrial and Corporate Change*, 14, 3: 1–42.

Lazonick, W. and Shin, J.-S., 2020. *Predatory Value Extraction: How the Looting of the Business Corporation Became the US Norm and How Sustainable Prosperity Can Be Restored*. Oxford University Press: Oxford.

Lazonick, W., and Tulum, Ö., 2011. 'US biopharmaceutical finance and the sustainability of the biotech business model', *Research Policy*, 40, 9: 1170–87.

Lazonick, W., Sakınç, M., and Hopkins, M., 2020. 'Why stock buybacks are dangerous for the economy', *Harvard Business Review*, 7 January, https:// hbr.org/2020/01/why-stock-buybacks-are-dangerous-for-the-economy? ab=hero-subleft-.

Lazonick, W., Hopkins, M., Jacobson, K., Sakınç, M., and Tulum, Ö., 2017. 'U.S. pharma's business model: Why it is broken, and how it can be fixed', in Tyfield, D., Lave, R., Randalls, S. and Thorpe, C. eds., *The Routledge Handbook of the Political Economy of Science*, Taylor & Francis: London: 83–100.

Lazonick, W., Tulum, Ö., Hopkins, M., Sakınç, M., and Jacobson, K., 2019. 'Financialization of the U.S. pharmaceutical industry', Institute for New Economic Thinking Working Paper, 2 December, https://www.ineteco nomics.org/perspectives/blog/financialization-us-pharma-industry.

Liu, A., 2021. 'The top 10 biopharma M&A deals in 2020', *Fierce Pharma*, 19 January, https://www.fiercepharma.com/special-report/top-10-largest-bio pharma-m-a-deals-2020.

McNamee, L. and Ledley, F., 2013. 'Assessing the history and value of Human Genome Sciences', *Journal of Commercial Biotechnology*, 19, 4: 3–10.

Montalban, M., and Sakınç, M., 2013. 'Financialization and productive models in the pharmaceutical industry', *Industrial and Corporate Change*, 22, 4: 981–1030.

Morgan, P., Brown, D., Lennard, S. et al., 2018. 'Impact of a five-dimensional framework on R&D productivity at AstraZeneca', *Nature Reviews Drug Discovery*, 17, 3: 167–81.

Mullard, A., 2019. 'An audience with Hal Barron: News & analysis', *Nature Reviews Drug Discovery*, 18, 3: 166–7.

Murphey, R., 2020. 'Top biotech venture capital funds of 2018–2021', *Bay Bridge Bio*, 27 May, www.baybridgebio.com/blog/top_vcs_2018.html.

Murphy, K., 1999. 'Executive compensation', in Ashenfelter, O. and Card, D. eds., *Handbook of Labor Economics*, North Holland: Amsterdam: 2485–2563.

Neville, S. 2017. 'GSK chief vows to stop "drifting off in hobbyland" with R&D'. *Financial Times,* 6 August, *https://www.ft.com/content/93055876-76cf-11e7-90c0-90a9d1bc9691.*

O'Sullivan, E., Andreoni, A., Lopez-Gomez, C. and Gregory, M., 2013. 'What is new in the new industrial policy? A manufacturing systems perspective', *Oxford Review of Economic Policy*, 29, 2: 432–62.

Owen, G., and Hopkins, M., 2016. *Science, the State and the City: Britain's Struggle to Succeed in Biotechnology*, Oxford University Press: Oxford.

Palladino, L., 2018. 'The $1 trillion question: New approaches to regulating stock buybacks', *Yale Journal of Regulation*, 36: 89–105, https://www.yalejreg.com/bulletin/the-1-trillion-question-new-approaches-to-regulating-stock-buybacks-2/.

Pfizer, 2020. 'Event brief of Q4 2019 Pfizer Inc earnings call – final', *CQ FD Disclosure*, 28 January.

Pisani, B., 2021. 'Buybacks are poised for a record year, but who do they help?' *CNBC*, 30 December, www.cnbc.com/2021/12/30/buybacks-are-poised-for-a-record-year-but-who-do-they-help.html.

Pisano, G., 2006. *Science Business: The Promise, the Reality, and the Future of Biotech*. Harvard Business School Press: Boston.

Pollack, A., 2007. 'AstraZeneca buys MedImmune for $15.6 billion', *New York Times*, 24 April, https://www.nytimes.com/2007/04/24/business/24drug-web.html.

Pratley, N., 2012. 'Shareholder spring is offering even more sport than usual'. *The Guardian*, 17 May, https://www.theguardian.com/business/2012/may/17/shareholder-spring-investor-revolt-pay.

Quirke, V., and Slinn, J., 2010. 'Perspectives on twentieth-century pharmaceuticals: An introduction', in Quirke, V., and Slinn, J. eds., *Perspectives on Twentieth-Century Pharmaceuticals*, Peter Lang: Oxford: 1–34.

Rafols, I., Hopkins, M., Hoekman, J. et al., 2014. 'Big pharma, little science?: A bibliometric perspective on big pharma's R&D decline', *Technological Forecasting and Social Change*, 81: 22–38.

Randles, S., 2002. 'Complex systems applied? The merger that made GlaxoSmithKline', *Technology Analysis & Strategic Management*, 14, 3: 331–54.

Reuters Staff, 2022. 'GSK workers vote to strike over pay dispute', *Reuters*, 20 April, www.reuters.com/article/gsk-strike/gsk-workers-vote-to-strike-over-pay-dispute-idUSL3N2WI2JC.

Romeo, V., 2015. 'Neil Woodford launches fresh attack on GlaxoSmithKline', *Money Marketing*, 20 November, www.moneymarketing.co.uk/news/neil-woodford-launches-fresh-attack-on-glaxosmithkline/.

Sainsbury, D., 2020. *Windows of Opportunity: How Nations Create Value.* Profile Books: London.

Sakınç, M., 2017. 'Share repurchases in Europe: A value extraction analysis', ISIGrowth Working Paper 16, 17 June, www.isigrowth.eu/2017/06/15/share-repurchases-in-europe-a-value-extraction-analysis/.

Saul, S. and Pollack, A., 2008. 'Bristol-Myers offers $4.5 billion for rest of ImClone', *New York Times*, 31 July, www.nytimes.com/2008/07/31/business/worldbusiness/31iht-01bristol.14924451.html.

Stahl, L., 2021. 'Chip shortage highlights U.S. dependence on fragile supply chain', *60 Minutes*, 2 May, www.cbsnews.com/news/semiconductor-chip-shortage-60-minutes-2021-05-02/.

Stone, P., 2013. 'The vulture-fund billionaire is the GOP's go-to guy on Wall Street', *Mother Jones*, September/October, https://www.motherjones.com/politics/2013/10/paul-singer-elliott-republican-fundraiser/.

Timmons, H., 2003. 'Glaxo shareholders revolt against pay plan for chief', *New York Times*, 20 May, www.nytimes.com/2003/05/20/business/glaxo-shareholders-revolt-against-pay-plan-for-chief.html.

Tulum, Ö., 2018. 'Innovation and financialization in the US biopharmaceutical industry', Unpublished doctoral dissertation, *Faculty of Economics, University of Ljubljana*, June, http://www.cek.ef.uni-lj.si/doktor/tulum.pdf.

Tulum, Ö., and Lazonick, W., 2018. 'Financialized corporations in a national innovation system: The U.S. pharmaceutical industry', *International Journal of Political Economy*, 47: 3–4: 281–316.

Tulum, Ö., Lazonick, W., Jacobson, K., and Chappelka, E., 2021. 'Who controls the supply of COVID-19 vaccines, and why does it matter?' Academic-Industry Research Network, 21 September, https://theairnet.org/12-who-controls-the-supply-of-covid-19-vaccines-and-why-does-it-matter/.

Ward, A., 2015. 'GlaxoSmithKline: Out of step. In an interview, Andrew Witty, GSK's embattled chief executive makes the case for his new strategy', *Financial Times*, 11 May, https://www.ft.com/content/3a7f8df0-f7b7-11e4-9beb-00144feab7de.

Weintraub, A. 2018. 'GlaxoSmithKline CEO reshuffles 40% of management team in bid to bring in new ideas', *Fierce Pharma,* 18 January, https://www

.fiercepharma.com/corporate/glaxosmithkline-ceo-reshuffles-40-manage
ment-team-bid-to-bring-new-ideas

Wild, L., 2016. 'Woodford slams "madness" at GlaxoSmithKline', *Interactive Investor*, 24 February, www.ii.co.uk/analysis-commentary/woodford-slams-madness-glaxosmithkline-ii297324.

Woodford, N., 2017. 'GLAXIT', *Woodford Funds Blog*, 12 May.

Woodruff, D., 2002. 'Barnevik resigns from Investor AB amid controversy over ABB payout', *Wall Street Journal*, 15 February, https://www.wsj.com/art icles/SB1013722522573212600.

23andMe, 2021. 'DNS genetic testing for health, ancestry and more.' *Retrieved 6 March, 2021, from* https://www.23andme.com/

Acknowledgements

The research has been funded primarily by the Gatsby Foundation at the Department of Economics of SOAS University of London.[*] We thank Lord David Sainsbury for his intellectual engagement with this study.

Additional funding was provided by the Institute for New Economic Thinking and the Canadian Institute for Advanced Research through the Academic-Industry Research Network. We would like to thank Marie Carpenter, Matt Hopkins, and Erdem Sakınç for their involvement in our broader study of the relationships between corporate governance and economic performance in the United Kingdom. We would also like to thank people who read and commented on earlier versions of this study, including Rosie Collington, Thomas Ferguson, Pauline Gleadle, Colin Haslam, Geoffrey Owen, and Els Torreele.

---

[*] *Governing Financialisation, Innovation and Productivity in UK Manufacturing, GOFINPRO Research Programme, Gatsby Grant Number: GAT3597.*

Cambridge Elements ≡

Reinventing Capitalism

Arie Y. Lewin

Duke University

Arie Y. Lewin is Professor Emeritus of Strategy and International Business at Duke University, Fuqua School of Business. He is an Elected Fellow of the Academy of International Business and a Recipient of the Academy of Management inaugural Joanne Martin Trailblazer Award. Previously, he was Editor-in-Chief of *Management and Organization Review* (2015–2021) and the *Journal of International Business Studies* (2000–2007), founding Editor-in-Chief of *Organization Science* (1989–2007), and Convener of Organization Science Winter Conference (1990–2012). His research centers on studies of organizations' adaptation as co-evolutionary systems, the emergence of new organizational forms, and adaptive capabilities of innovating and imitating organizations. His current research focuses on de-globalization and decoupling, the Fourth Industrial Revolution, and the renewal of capitalism.

Till Talaulicar

University of Erfurt

Till Talaulicar holds the Chair of Organization and Management at the University of Erfurt where he is also the Dean of the Faculty of Economics, Law and Social Sciences. His main research expertise is in the areas of corporate governance and the responsibilities of the corporate sector in modern societies. Professor Talaulicar is Editor-in-Chief of Corporate Governance: An International Review, Senior Editor of Management and Organization Review and serves on the Editorial Board of Organization Science. Moreover, he has been Founding Member and Chairperson of the Board of the International Corporate Governance Society (2014–2020).

About the Series

This series seeks to feature explorations about the crisis of legitimacy facing capitalism today, including the increasing income and wealth gap, the decline of the middle class, threats to employment due to globalization and digitalization, undermined trust in institutions, discrimination against minorities, global poverty and pollution. Being grounded in a business and management perspective, the series incorporates contributions from multiple disciplines on the causes of the current crisis and potential solutions to renew capitalism.

Panmure House is the final and only remaining home of Adam Smith, Scottish philosopher and 'Father of modern economics.' Smith occupied the House between 1778 and 1790, during which time he completed the final editions of his master works: The Theory of Moral Sentiments and The Wealth of Nations. Other great luminaries and thinkers of the Scottish Enlightenment visited Smith regularly at the House across this period. Their mission is to provide a world-class twenty-first-century centre for social and economic debate and research, convening in the name of Adam Smith to effect positive change and forge global, future-focussed networks.

Cambridge Elements ☰

Reinventing Capitalism

Printed in the United States
by Baker & Taylor Publisher Services